The Only Empath And Narcissist Bible

Mastering the Balance of Empathy and Self-Protection. How to Shield Yourself from Manipulation, Understand Narcissistic Behaviors, and Cultivating Healthy Relationships.

WHITNEY BARTON

© **Copyright 2024 - All rights reserved.**

The content inside this book may not be duplicated, reproduced, or transmitted without direct written permission from the author or publisher.

Under no circumstances will any blame or legal responsibility be held against the publisher, or author, for any damages, reparation, or monetary loss due to the information contained within this book, either directly or indirectly.

Legal Notice:

This book is copyright protected. It is only for personal use. You cannot amend, distribute, sell, use, quote or paraphrase any part, or the content within this book, without the consent of the author or publisher.

Disclaimer Notice:

Please note the information contained within this document is for educational and entertainment purposes only. All effort has been executed to present accurate, reliable, up to date, complete information. No warranties of any kind are declared or implied. Readers acknowledge that the author is not engaging in the rendering of legal, financial, medical, or professional advice. The content within this book has been derived from various sources. Please consult a licensed professional before attempting any techniques outlined in this book.

By reading this document, the reader agrees that under no circumstances is the author responsible for any losses, direct or indirect, that are incurred as a result of the use of the information contained within this document, including, but not limited to, errors, omissions, or inaccuracies.

TABLE OF CONTENTS

INTRODUCTION	5
CHAPTER ONE: The Empath And The Narcissist	**7**
Empathy vs. Narcissism: Understanding the Duality	*8*
Opposites Attract: How Empaths and Narcissists Interact	*12*
Dysfunctions of the Empath-Narcissist Dynamic	*14*
CHAPTER TWO: Understanding The Empath	**17**
Compassion, Intuition, Sensitivity, Emotional Intelligence: What Makes an Empath Unique	*18*
The Many Gifts of Being an Empath	*21*
The Empath Wound: How Feeling Too Much Makes You Vulnerable	*24*
CHAPTER THREE: Understanding The Narcissist	**28**
Narcissism and Its Spectrum	*30*
Exploring the Narcissist's Core Motivation	*34*
Recognizing Red Flags: Common Narcissistic Tactics and Traits	*37*
CHAPTER FOUR: The Art Of Setting Healthy Boundaries	**43**
Importance of Boundaries for Empaths	*45*
Effective Techniques for Setting Clear and Firm Boundaries with Narcissists	*48*
Boundary-Setting Visualization Exercise for Empaths	*53*
Dealing with Repeat Boundary Violations	*54*
CHAPTER FIVE: Emotional Self-Defense: Shielding Your Energy	**58**
Practicing Emotional Distancing in Interactions with Narcissists	*59*
Energy Shielding: Exercises for Grounding and Protection	*63*
Recognizing and Avoiding Energy Vampires	*68*
CHAPTER SIX: The Narcissist In Your Life: Handling Different Relationships	**72**
Narcissism Manifestation in Different Relationships	*72*
Power of Interdependence: Cultivating Healthy, Fulfilling Relationships	*79*
CHAPTER SEVEN: Healing And Recovering From Narcissistic Abuse	**82**
The Emotional and Psychological Impact	*83*
Rebuilding Self-Esteem through Self-Compassion	*85*
How to Heal from Gaslighting and Emotional Abuse	*91*
CHAPTER EIGHT: Self-Care: Nurturing Your Empathic Soul	**94**
Best Self-Care Practices for Well-Being	*96*
Managing Overwhelm to Prevent Empathy Burnout	*99*
Healthy Coping Mechanisms	*101*
CHAPTER NINE: Developing Resilience Against Setbacks And Failures	**105**
Resilience Worksheet	*107*

CONCLUSION 110

INTRODUCTION

Have you ever found yourself feeling utterly drained after spending time with certain individuals? Does it seem like you absorb the emotions of others effortlessly, leaving you both invigorated and utterly exhausted? Perhaps you've experienced the frustration of pouring your heart into a relationship, only to find your efforts met with an insatiable need for validation or attention.

These encounters might just be indicative of something deeper within you – an innate ability to keenly sense and share the emotions of those around you. You could very well be what's commonly referred to as an empath.

Yet, as beautiful as the gift of empathy can be, it comes with its own set of challenges. The world is not always kind, and sometimes empathy can leave you vulnerable to manipulation and exploitation, especially when dealing with individuals who lack empathy themselves, such as narcissists. These individuals, often charming and charismatic on the surface, are driven solely by their own desires and needs, often at the expense of others. Thus, the empath-narcissist dynamic becomes a delicate and potentially harmful dance.

The Only Empath and Narcissist Bible is your comprehensive guide to understanding this dynamic.

This book is more than just a self-help manual. It explores the very essence of who you are as an empath, highlighting your unique strengths and vulnerabilities. You'll gain a deeper understanding of narcissism, its spectrum, and the tactics narcissists use to gain control. But most importantly, this book gives you the tools to protect yourself and cultivate healthy relationships.

It is more than just a book, though. Think of it as a bible that sets you on the path to self-discovery, healing, recovery, and thriving. As you begin reading, remember that you aren't alone. Mastering the balance between empathy and self-protection will help you build fulfilling relationships as you live a life of compassion and resilience.

CHAPTER ONE:
The Empath And The Narcissist

These days, it's not easy dating or being in a relationship – what with all the e-dating, catfishing, ghosting, etc. happening. Imagine dating someone new and believing you're both in love. You think the world of this person but also feel like there's something amiss. Your new partner appears to be different from you in so many ways. But the difference infuses you with a sense of excitement. Every text from this person made butterflies dance in your tummy. They are charming, funny, and always have the right words for you.

On dates, they always have extravagant compliments and gestures that make you blush. Yet, your stomach has an unsettling feeling whenever you're together. Your partner needs constant reassurance, and their compliments feel like veiled criticism of you and your style. As the relationship progresses, you begin to notice things you didn't see from the jump. For instance, you rarely talk about yourself during conversations because the topic is usually centered on this person. You find yourself apologizing for trivial things and must walk on eggshells around them.

Conversations cause plenty of arguments that leave you feeling drained. You start to suspect this person may not be who you think they are. After much thought, you find yourself wondering if you're in a relationship with a narcissist. Was this the intense love you craved, or was it something else entirely? You open your phone to google "empath" and "narcissist," the unsettling feeling in your gut getting stronger as you recognize the troubling parallels.

Not in your wildest dreams would you think this was possible, but here you are – in love with a narcissist.

The empath and the narcissist are polar opposites. Yet, they tend to attract each other and end up in romantic relationships together. Sadly, the result is often disastrous for the empath. Given their distinct personalities and natural tendencies, the empath gives while the narcissist takes – until the empath has nothing left to give.

You're here to learn as much as possible about the empath and the narcissist, most likely to protect yourself. So, in this chapter, I will take you on a journey to understand the empath-narcissist dynamic.

Who is the empath? Who is the narcissist? Why are they attracted to each other? And more importantly, why is this attraction dangerous to the empath? What are the challenges of the empath-narcissist dynamic?

These are the questions you will find answers to in this first chapter. By the end, you should know more than the basics about empaths and narcissists and the basis of their attraction.

Let's begin by examining the duality of empathy and narcissism.

Empathy vs. Narcissism: Understanding the Duality

Empathy is commonly defined as the ability to emotionally understand another person's feelings, see things from their perspective, and put yourself in their shoes. In other words, empathy is imagining yourself in someone else's position and mirroring what they feel in any situation.

The Merriam-Webster dictionary defines empathy as "the action of understanding, being aware of, being sensitive to, and vicariously experiencing the feelings, thoughts, and experience of another of either the past or present without having the feelings, thoughts, and experience fully communicated in an objectively explicit manner."

Here's what this definition means in simpler terms:

- **"Understanding and being aware"**: You know what someone else is feeling and thinking, even if they don't tell you.
- **"Being sensitive"**: You pick up on their emotional cues, like how plants sense sunlight.
- **"Vicariously experiencing"**: You don't feel exactly as they feel, but you get a taste of it. Imagine watching a sad movie and feeling a little down as a result.

The last part of the definition means you don't need the person to tell you their whole story to know and understand how they feel. Rather, you pick up on their emotions through words, actions, body language, or facial expressions.

When you see a person in distress, you can immediately see yourself experiencing the same thing and embody what they're going through.

For example, if you meet someone who has just lost a loved one, you can imagine what it would feel like to lose your own loved one and thus empathize with this person's grief.

Being able to get into other people's heads is much more difficult than attuning to your own emotions and feelings. Empathy enables you to "walk a mile in others' shoes," so to say. It lets you understand the feelings another person is experiencing at any given moment.

Humans need empathy to relate and cooperate. There's no humanity without it. When you empathize, you not only feel what the other person is feeling but are moved to help. In other words, empathy prompts us to care for one another.

The distress you feel from seeing others suffer is the seed of the compassion that stems from empathy. No one always empathizes; some people have a significantly higher degree of empathy than others.

For the average person, seeing a suffering person and responding with indifference or blatant hostility appears incomprehensible. However, some people do respond in this way, which tells us that empathy isn't necessarily a universal experience or response. And that's where narcissism comes in.

Narcissism, in short, is a disorder of lack of empathy. Individuals with high-degree narcissism show little to no interest in others' well-being, almost to the point of neglect. Science doesn't yet entirely understand what causes some people to be capable of seriously harming another human being. But when empathy is "turned off" and a person operates entirely on an "I" basis. That is, they view the world as though they are the only ones who exist or matter. Such a person with an "I exist, you don't" mindset is more inclined to disregard other people's feelings and needs. This is the mindset narcissism breeds.

Our ability to empathize is affected by our genetic makeup, childhood and upbringing, social environment, age, emotional maturity, and physical and mental well-being. Also, this ability isn't fixed. At this moment, you might feel incredibly empathetic toward someone else, but feelings of irritability or anger can impair your ability to feel the same level of empathy in another moment.

The scientific understanding is that empathy develops in the context of care right from infancy. As an infant, you smile and cry to get your primary caregiver to cater to your needs. The first type of empathy we experience as infants is the ability to unconsciously mimic someone else's emotions. Experts call this emotional contagion, and it is believed to be an innate ability.

Emotional contagion is observed, for instance, when two infants giggle along with each other contagiously. Empathy originates early from this prototype as long as a child reaches normal developmental milestones.

Many theorists hypothesize that individuals with severe narcissistic traits exhibit a form of "developmental arrest," This is marked by an inability to internalize a stable and positive sense of self. Additionally, they lack the coping mechanisms needed to maintain this self-image in the face of inevitable disappointments and challenges in life.

In other words, normal functioning people experienced numerous instances of being validated and admired by their primary caregivers, whereas the narcissistic person didn't. Thus, the lack of empathy that highly narcissistic people display is the inevitable consequence of having been insufficiently catered to and validated by their primary caregivers in childhood.

Empathy is multifaceted. It involves cognitive and affective understanding of someone else's emotional state. It also consists of being able to monitor yourself and regulate Self-Other awareness. Compared to processes like sympathy, empathy is the ability to separate yourself from others and recognize alternative perspectives and potential emotions.

There are two main components of empathy:
- **Cognitive empathy** is knowing what someone else feels and what they might be thinking in any situation. We also call this perspective-taking. Individuals who fall within the Dark Triad—narcissists, Machiavellians, and Sociopaths—experience this type of empathy without feeling their victims' emotions.
- **Affective empathy:** Also known as emotional empathy, this is when you feel just as the other person feels. It enables you to attune to the person's emotional state. Your own experiences of emotions allow you to feel along with them. Suppose a person's range of feelings is limited. In that case, they may have difficulty recognizing emotions they can't readily access or process themselves in others. This is what happens with narcissists. Conversely, an empath has an expansive range of emotions to draw upon to effectively empathize with others.

From this, it becomes clear that empaths understand others' emotions on a cognitive and affective level. In contrast, narcissists understand only on a mental level. This makes narcissists incapable of experiencing other aspects of empathy, such as compassion, remorse, etc. As a result, they can manipulate and exploit others to their advantage. Meanwhile, empathy nurtures connection and support, making building and maintaining meaningful relationships easier.

The duality of empathy and narcissism can create a ripple effect on the interpersonal dynamics between people with high degrees of each trait, i.e., empaths and narcissists.

What does this mean? You're about to find out.

Opposites Attract: How Empaths and Narcissists Interact

Opposites attract. This is an old cliche, yet it's often true – especially with the most unlikely pairing. We consider cats and dogs natural enemies, but they've been known to live in the same household as domestic pets. You've probably seen a cat cozy up to a dog at one point. As have I and many others.

This cliche is also true for people with opposing personalities. Who would possibly think that an individual who feels and understands emotions so deeply that they can take on other people's feelings would be attracted to a self-absorbed, vain, and often grandiose person? Yet, this is the reality of the empath-narcissist dynamic. The empath and the narcissist are two contrasting personalities, but they somehow always find themselves in a complex interpersonal dynamic.

While the empath is a highly sensitive person with the ability to pick up on subtle, nonverbal cues about the emotions, feelings, and thoughts of anyone around them, the narcissist is characterized by a sense of inflated self-importance and a lack of empathy for others.

The empath is sensitive to the feelings and energies of those around them. As a result, they are inclined to put others' needs ahead of their own without doubt. The empath also struggles to set and enforce personal boundaries, which makes them take on other people's emotional burdens. They are compassionate and want to help others, but that makes them easy prey for the narcissist who's always on the lookout for someone to exploit.

The narcissist has an insatiable need for attention, admiration, and validation from everyone around them. With their inflated ego and faux sense of self-importance, they are quite difficult and draining to be around. Unfortunately, this makes an empath the perfect pairing for the narcissist—often to the former's detriment.

Narcissistic individuals have trouble empathizing with others on an emotional level. As such, they're incapable of experiencing and demonstrating empathy like empaths. They are often self-centered and manipulative, viewing the world solely through their perspective.

Despite their distinct personalities and traits, these two find themselves drawn to each other. There's usually an intense connection that inevitably shapes how they interact in interpersonal relationships, particularly romantic ones. Interactions between the empath and the narcissist tend to create negative relationship patterns that mainly harm the empath.

Though there isn't current scientific research investigating how empaths and narcissists interact, anecdotal evidence points to the existence of such relationships. This could be due to the narcissist's need for external affirmation and the tendency of the empath to provide such affirmation and validation.

Such a dynamic can be dysfunctional and unstable. The empath is more likely to forgive hurtful behavior, and the narcissist literally can't act any other way. Whether in platonic or romantic relationships, the dynamic creates a cycle of increasingly toxic behavior.

Empaths are givers, while narcissists are takers. Consequently, empaths and narcissists interact in an entirely one-sided way. The empath constantly gives, and the narcissist constantly takes. It's a perfect symbiotic relationship because each party is comfortable in their chosen role.

The empath feels responsible for taking care of the other party, so they work extra hard to meet all of the narcissist's needs. Conversely, the narcissist feels entitled to the empath's time, energy, words of affirmation, acts of service, and many more without ever reciprocating.

I'll share an example of how this dynamic plays out to help you better understand how the empath and the narcissist interact. In this case, Viola is the empath, and Max is the narcissist.

When Viola and Max meet, she is instantly taken by Max's charm and humor. He is confident, attractive, and dashing. But over time, as Max's need for validation and attention becomes apparent, Viola deals with increasing demands and criticisms. Though Viola recognizes that there's something amiss, her hyper-awareness of

Max's emotional state makes it incredibly difficult to end the relationship or enforce her boundaries.

The bottom line is that the empath and the narcissist are drawn to each other because 1) the empath has a lot of compassion and affection to give, and 2) the narcissist thrives on being worshipped. But they don't make a good match because the empath is inclined to always forgive the narcissist – no matter how bad their behavior gets.

Thus, the empath-narcissist interactions result in the empath being completely exploited and disregarded, as the narcissist causes more and more chaos.

As one might expect, the empath-narcissist dynamic has plenty of downsides. In fact, there are hardly any upsides for the empath. Both personality types are drawn toward each other for all the wrong reasons, leading to a catastrophic end for the empath.

Let's look at what this means.

Dysfunctions of the Empath-Narcissist Dynamic

The attraction between empaths and narcissists is a toxic one destined for disaster. The narcissist sees in the empath a loving, giving person who will be devoted to them and worship them. But sadly, the empath is attracted to the narcissist due to the narcissist's presentation of a false self. In other words, the narcissist approaches the empath by presenting a false self in which they seem charming, intelligent, confident, and even giving.

In the early phase, when the narcissist is trying to reel the empath in, they present as attentive and loving. Soon, though, the mask begins slowly coming off – especially as the empath becomes comfortable in the relationship. In the early phase, the narcissist only sees the positive qualities of their new victim. And because they're in the relationship to look good, that makes them happy and loving. But this doesn't last because the narcissist has a faux sense of superiority and thinks everyone else is beneath them. Once they notice the empath's flaws, they stop idealizing and start berating them for being imperfect.

Usually, it takes a while for the narcissist's true colors to show, so the best thing you can do is never to fall in love with one. However, this doesn't work for the empath who believes they can fix and heal anyone with compassion. It's difficult for many empaths to even conceive that many people are incapable of experiencing empathy.

While the empath works for harmony, the narcissist loves drama and chaos. They relish in their ability to pull others' strings. Narcissists string empaths along with false, intermittent hope. They know how to incorporate kindness and compliments into their dysfunctional behavior, so much so that they convince their victim that behaving appropriately is the key to getting the loving person they once knew.

Empaths tend to understand humanity – they know we all have flaws and are willing to help others through their personal growth. As such, they will be long-suffering if a narcissist says, "I know I'm not perfect, I really want to change." Narcissists have moments where they (manipulatively) admit their fault but never really follow through on addressing it. This tactic is merely used to reel the empath back in. It's effective with empaths because they only want to support and help the narcissist grow. Unfortunately, it only leads to further exploitation.

The empath-narcissist dynamic has a push-and-pull nature that almost always creates a trauma bond between victim and abuser. For the empath, it can feel impossible to end the relationship, regardless of how much it's harming them. With the highly sensitive nature comes the empath's ability and willingness to examine themselves and their faults. That tends to get taken advantage of as the trauma bond strengthens.

It creates a cycle where the trauma-bonded empath starts looking at themselves and determining what they must change or do differently and what flaws they must address to keep the relationship going.

The narcissist's greatest weapon in this dynamic is to turn the empath against themselves. Using specific techniques, they underhandedly attack and destroy the empath's mental health from the inside out.

First, the narcissist continually invalidates the empath's feelings. Eventually, the empath starts to doubt most of their thoughts, feelings, and reality. Then, the narcissist distorts the empath's introspectiveness and empathy, convincing them they are flaws rather than gifts. Ultimately, the narcissist infiltrates the empath's life to sabotage it by acting like they care.

You can only survive such an attack if you're aware of the manipulation tactics and techniques narcissists use. That way, you can escape before your sense of self becomes compromised.

This was only meant to provide some basic insights into how the empath-narcissist dynamic operates. Now that you have some idea, we will dive in even deeper by examining each personality type individually.

In the next chapter, you will learn who an empath is, what makes them unique, if you're an empath, and why empaths are vulnerable to narcissists. By the end, you will know much more about empaths than you currently do.

So, keep reading!

CHAPTER TWO:
Understanding The Empath

Picture a vibrant world where emotions come in colors and shades. For instance, happiness could be a sunny yellow, anger a fiery red, and sadness a deep hue of blue. Now, imagine empaths as special butterflies with transparent wings. They have emotional colors that are ever-changing. But when they're around people, their see-through wings take on the colors of everyone else's feelings.

When an empath enters a crowded room, they might experience a mix of emotions—such as the nervousness of a person on a first date (pale green), the tension between friends (dark gray), and the calm of an elderly couple (soft lavender).

In a different situation, when an empath is with a friend who is really sad (deep blue), the empath feels sad, too, but with a twist. They absorb some of the sadness, making the friend feel a bit lighter. They may not be able to completely get rid of the feeling. Still, they can offer more comfort than the average person.

Though not an official term in psychology, empaths are generally people who are highly attuned to other people's feelings and emotions. The word empath comes from the word "empathy," which is why I started this book by dissecting the concept of empathy itself.

Empaths are empaths because they can soak up the emotions of people around them, whether good or bad. In the book The Empath's Survival Guide: Life Strategies for Sensitive People, Judith Orloff, MD, a pioneer in this field, says empaths absorb the joys and stress of their environments like "emotional sponges."

According to Orloff, empaths lack the filtration system most people use to shield themselves from overstimulation. This makes them vulnerable to the affective states of everyone around them. As a result, they can't avoid taking in surrounding feelings and energies, whether good, bad, or in between.

Empaths are extremely sensitive to external stimuli, including domineering personalities, chaotic environments, and sounds. They feel everything very deeply. But not all empaths soak up every feeling they come across. Those trained can choose which emotions to absorb, just as butterflies choose the flowers they land on. These experienced empaths can handle emotionally challenging situations without getting overwhelmed.

Now, though empaths can sense what a person is feeling or thinking, they aren't mind readers. Even if they know someone's upset, they don't know why. They still have to talk things out to understand the why. Also, empaths enjoy helping others but can't "fix" people no matter how hard they try. They're gifted at understanding and being supportive – sometimes to their detriment.

You learned briefly about empaths in the first chapter. Now, we're about to look at what it means to be one. Understanding what being an empath entails is necessary to protect yourself, especially from narcissists. If you're an empath, you're vulnerable to emotional overwhelm. So, being in a negative or toxic relationship can drain the very soul out of you. That's why you must learn as much as possible about the strengths and limitations of being an empath.

Here, I will show you what makes empaths unique and the many gifts you possess. More importantly, we will discuss how your core wound (all empaths have this) may be leaving you vulnerable to narcissists and other emotional vampires.

We'll begin by answering this question: What makes an empath unique? In other words, why are you special? Let's find out.

Compassion, Intuition, Sensitivity, Emotional Intelligence: What Makes an Empath Unique

Most people are naturally capable of empathy, but it exists on a spectrum. An empath is on the more extreme end of this spectrum, which means they experience a more intense form of empathy. This ability to take on the affective state of others sets empaths apart from regular people with regular empathy levels. It is one of the things that makes empaths unique. But other traits also make them unique, and we'll look at those now.

Before we talk about that, though, the following are indicators that you're an empath.

- You're good at listening to and understanding others.
- People feel comfortable confiding in you.
- You're adept at picking up on nonverbal cues about how others feel.
- People often come to you for advice.
- You feel overwhelmed by emotionally tasking media.
- You get the strong urge to help when you see someone suffering.
- You can tell when people are being insincere.
- Social situations overwhelm and drain you.
- You care deeply about others.
- Tragic events overwhelm you.
- You struggle to set boundaries in interpersonal relationships.

If people often say you're too emotional or sensitive, that could be a sign. Also, you may have noticed that you feel drained after spending time around certain people.

There are many upsides to being an empath. First, you're a superb listener, which makes you an excellent friend. You are also likely to consistently show up for friends who need your help. You're emotionally intelligent, highly intuitive, big-hearted, and generous.

But the same qualities that make you such a fantastic person can be hard on you. Since you quite literally absorb others' feelings, you can become overwhelmed by their emotions – particularly the negative ones like anger and anxiety. You may also take on other people's problems as yours. Due to the inability to set boundaries, you may find it hard to say no, even when others ask too much of you. Crowds, in particular, can be overwhelming because you're extra sensitive to noise and nonstop chatter. As such, you may feel at your best when surrounded by nature.

To determine whether you're an empath or not, answer these questions:

- If a friend is distressed, do I start feeling distraught, too?
- Do people call me "overly sensitive" or "too emotional"?
- Are my feelings easy to hurt?
- Do I feel emotionally drained in crowds, often to the point where I need alone time to recharge?
- Do I overeat to cope when overwhelmed?
- Am I sensitive to noise, smells, and excessive chatter?

According to Judith Orloff, MD, answering "yes" to at least three questions means you're likely an empath. And if you answer "yes" to more than three, that makes you an empath. Recognizing yourself as an empath is crucial in taking control of your emotions instead of drowning in them all the time.

Now, what makes you unique?

As an empath, you have a special set of traits from your profound sensitivity to others' emotions and energies. This increased awareness and sensitivity makes you unique in many ways:

You're an intuitive master

Being an empath means you have the gift of intuition. Everyone is intuitive on some level, but your intuition is on a whole different level. It gives you the ability to sense uncommunicated emotions and intentions. You can pick up on nonverbal cues, including body language and microexpressions, no matter how subtle. This makes you a natural at seeing beneath the surface. Your exceptional intuition makes you an excellent listener and confidante, making people see you as a safe space to express their vulnerabilities and find emotional support.

Let's say you're a college student working on a group project. You notice that one of your team members, Paige, seems quiet and withdrawn. There are subtle cues in her body language and face – a slight tremor in her hands and a downturned mouth. You sense that Paige is probably anxious about the looming project deadline. Going with your gut, you gently approach Paige after a team meeting. "Hey Paige, everything alright? You seem a little stressed lately." This allows her to confide in you, enabling you to comfort and reassure her.

You're incredibly compassionate

Your intuitive nature, combined with your deep understanding of emotional states, results in a strong sense of compassion and care for the people in your life. You're genuinely concerned for others' well-being and feel compelled to alleviate their suffering in any way you can. As such, you're a natural at nurturing people and bringing comfort to those in need.

You're extremely sensitive to emotional overload

But your very strengths act as double-edged swords. The constant influx of emotions leaves you vulnerable to overload. Negative and intense situations and crowded environments can be extremely draining for you. Are you familiar with the feeling of constantly getting bombarded with information? That's what being an empath in emotionally charged situations feels like.

You're uniquely perceptive

Though we're all empathetic, empaths take it to an extraordinary level. As an empath, your sensitivity goes beyond understanding how others feel. You can feel those emotions as though they were yours. Due to this, it may be hard to separate your feelings from the ones you pick up on in the surroundings. You need healthy coping mechanisms to regulate this unique perception.

Protecting yourself from taking on people's emotions can be difficult and nearly impossible. Still, it's achievable with healthy boundaries and quality self-care practices. However, suppose you lack the tools to manage the emotional "noise" around you. In that case, it can lead to significant distress in the long term.

Along the way, I will share comprehensive information on the tools you need to insulate yourself. So, that's another thing you can look forward to. For now, allow me to share with you the many gifts of being an empath.

The Many Gifts of Being an Empath

There's something uniquely special about being an empath. It goes beyond ordinary empathy or sympathy. It's about having a gift for perceiving and maneuvering the world in a way that the average person can't.

Psychologists have had plenty to say about the remarkable gift of being an empath. As it turns out, you possess some incredible gifts.

Here are these gifts:

- **A deep connection to nature**

Have you ever felt a powerful connection to the natural world? It's almost as if you can feel the very rhythm of the earth. You could walk through the woods and feel a rush of calm and peace. The birdsong, the scent of damp earth, the rustling leaves – everything resonates with you on a deeper level.

As an empath, you inherently understand that nature is to be explored and cherished. You don't just see it; you feel and connect with it. Your deep connection to nature can be a strong source of nourishment for your soul and spirit. This gift allows you to embrace harmony in an often chaotic world.

Suppose you're a city dweller who craves the calm and peace of nature. After a long week at work, you escape to a nearby forest for the weekend. Amidst the trees and sounds of nature, you feel the tension in your body melt away. Your connection to nature allows you to ground yourself and recharge your energy.

- **A capacity for profound relationships**

The capacity for profound and meaningful relationships is one of the many gifts of being an empath. This gift means you don't seek surface-level interactions with others. Instead, you're interested in connections that touch your very soul. This gift is a rewarding aspect of empathy because it is why empaths excel at acting as safe spaces for others. You don't just listen with your ears but with your heart. And though it can be emotionally taxing, the connections you form and the relationships you build are priceless.

Take my niece Gwen, for example. Gwen is an empath, which we're all very proud of. Recently, she observed a new student sitting alone at lunch at school. Others don't bat an eye, but Gwen feels sad for the isolated student. So, she walks over, introduces herself, and starts a conversation with the student. Her genuine interest and ability to sense the student's anxiety allowed Gwen to create a safe space for them to connect. I don't know more yet, but this small empathy act could blossom into a long-term friendship.

- **A unique relationship with solitude**

I know this sounds counterintuitive. After all, aren't you supposed to spend time connecting with others? True, but you also have the gift of solitude. You don't just enjoy having some alone time; you need it. Solitude allows you to recharge, process every emotion you've absorbed, and reconnect with yourself.

Humans need resilience to overcome the inevitable challenges and obstacles of life. As an empath, solitude is a crucial tool for developing this much-needed resilience. It's your sanctuary—a way to retreat from the emotional chatter of the world. And though some view solitude as aloof or antisocial, it's a valuable gift for empaths.

- **A gift of healing**

Empaths have a knack for healing that comes naturally. You don't just listen to people; you even help them chart a course to solve their problems. Whether they have a troubled mind, a wounded spirit, or a broken heart, you have a special gift for soothing and healing people. This doesn't necessarily mean you provide actionable solutions, but you understand people's pain and offer them comfort. Helping others to rediscover themselves and heal isn't just a privilege. One might even call it a calling. This profound gift is what makes you invaluable in friendships and relationships.

- **The gift of empathy**

This is the gift that defines you, so we must mention it once again. As an empath, you go beyond understanding people's feelings to experiencing them. It's what drives you to cheer for the joyful, comfort the suffering, and stand with anyone in between. The gift of empathy is your main gift, which you definitely wouldn't trade for anything in this world.

- **The power of presence**

The ability to be present – to be there for people and listen attentively without judgment – is another gift. It's a healing and validating gift. We live in a fast-paced world where there are plenty of things calling for attention at the same time. So, being able to offer people your undivided attention is a gift to that person. This gift means you can make anyone feel like they're the only person in the world, which is incredibly validating and comforting, particularly during challenging times.

Imagine a friend you can always count on. When you're sad, overwhelmed, frustrated, disappointed, etc., this friend puts down their phone, makes eye contact, and lets you talk while they listen with zero judgment. Their full presence empowers you to express your feelings freely, which makes you feel heard and validated. It also strengthens your bond.

These are some of the amazing gifts you possess as an empath. With them, you can make a difference in the lives of people around you and the world.

The Empath Wound: How Feeling Too Much Makes You Vulnerable

Although not recognized officially, "empath wound" refers to the vulnerability and pain empaths experience due to their extreme sensitivity to others' emotions and energies. It is a core issue that makes empaths vulnerable to specific people and situations.

As you've learned, empaths take on the emotions of people around them, often causing overload and exhaustion. For empaths who can't separate their feelings from other people's feelings, it can even lead to a loss of identity. The heightened sensitivity is both a gift and a curse because it lets empaths connect deeply to people but also leaves them susceptible to emotional trauma and stress.

In many cases, the empath wound has roots in childhood experiences. Let's say you were raised to prioritize the feelings and needs of others over yours. Then, you're likely to establish a pattern of neglecting your own emotions and needs in favor of helping others. Over time, you may develop a deep-seated belief that your needs and feelings are less important than those of others.

Also, being sensitive to your surroundings can be overwhelming, especially among people with intense or negative emotions. You may find yourself feeling anxious, depressed, or drained after spending time around specific people or in specific situations. This can be even worse if your core wound aligns with the negativity or trauma of the people or situations you encounter.

Because you're highly attuned to energies and emotions, you may subconsciously lean toward people who appear to be suffering. This can be a positive thing, but it can also steer you toward situations where you're exploited by vampires looking to drain your very soul of energy.

I mentioned that the struggle to distinguish your emotions from those you've absorbed can lead to identity loss. This can make it hard to set and enforce healthy personal boundaries in your interpersonal relationships. You may struggle to turn your "feel" button off and find it hard to stop giving, even when there's no energy left. Setting boundaries implies you don't care about people. You feel drained and burned out because you frequently put others ahead of yourself.

The question now is, how does the empath would make you vulnerable to narcissists in particular?

Well, the reason is that narcissists know how to take advantage of your empathy. They want someone who can give them undivided attention, admiration, and validation. You, on the other hand, see the narcissist as someone in need of understanding and support. Due to your inability to set boundaries and the narcissist's manipulative skills, you may find it hard to set limits in a relationship with them, leading to a cycle of manipulation and control.

The narcissist employs tools like love bombing, gaslighting, guilt-tripping, etc., in an attempt to manipulate and control you. Unfortunately, your heightened sensitivity makes you especially vulnerable to these tactics. As such, you may internalize the false narratives the narcissist feeds you and blame yourself for everything that goes wrong in your relationship. You don't realize it immediately, but this slowly chips at your sense of self and confidence.

To subdue and entrap you, the narcissist uses a cycle of idealization and devaluation. First, they show you attention, admiration, affection, and love (idealization). Then, they devalue you with verbal and sometimes non-verbal attacks. Eventually, there will be a third phase where they discard you once you no longer serve their needs.

The idealization phase can make you deeply attached to the narcissist because you're convinced they're your soulmate or kindred spirit. But when the devaluation phase inevitably begins, you may find it hard to let go. This is compounded by the false hope that you can restore the relationship to the earlier phase.

One thing that makes you susceptible to the narcissist's manipulation tactics is that you mirror the distress and trauma of their childhood. In other words, you can feel the narcissist's pain and suffering, which originates from their traumatic childhood.

The narcissist has a core wound stemming from deep-seated insecurity, inadequacy, and a frazzled sense of self. This wound develops in childhood due to neglect, abuse, or excessive indulgence without a genuine emotional bond with the primary caregiver. Any of these factors can make the narcissist create a grandiose self-image or false persona to install a facade over their innate feelings of unworthiness.

As an empath, you may see this wounded inner child living with the narcissist, leading to a strong urge to nurture and fix them. Consequently, you may feel compelled to "fix" or rescue them because you believe you can heal their wounds and transform them into a better person. You genuinely believe that the narcissist's emotional wound can be healed – that fixing them would lead to a deeper connection between both parties. The sense of obligation and responsibility alone can keep you entrapped in the dysfunctional relationship, even as it becomes increasingly damaging to you.

Slowly, though, you realize that the narcissist can't be fixed, healed, or rescued. Attempting to do that will only perpetuate the cycle of manipulation and control. And this further damages your physical, mental, emotional, and spiritual well-being.

To realize the extent of damage the narcissist can cause you, the next chapter will be a deep dive into understanding the narcissist. We will look at narcissism and the spectrum, discuss the narcissist's core wound in-depth, and teach you to recognize red flags that may point to an empath-narcissist dynamic in your relationships.

Get ready to peel back the layers of narcissism in a way that reveals not just ego but the inadequacies behind the facade of superiority and grandiosity.

CHAPTER THREE:
Understanding The Narcissist

We're in the internet and social media age. You know how hard many people work to curate their social media feeds meticulously. Individuals who are particular about social media ensure every post is a highlight reel – the fanciest meals, the best vacations, the wittiest jokes. They filter out anything that could ruin the "perfect" image they've carefully crafted on Instagram, TikTok, etc. Likes and comments act as validation – the more they get, the better.

This is precisely how narcissists view the world. Everyone around them is a follower to impress. Interactions are opportunities to share their curated image with people, not to form authentic connections. They only find others' accomplishments interesting if they can somehow tie them into their own narrative.

Here's the catch, though: Deep down, the narcissist's life isn't perfect. They have insecurities that they're hiding. However, admitting they're imperfect would only crack the outward facade. So, they do everything possible to maintain the charade, even if it makes them feel inauthentic and alone.

Now, most people on social media enjoy a curated online presence. The difference is that normal functioning people have a life outside that frame. Narcissists, on the other hand, are so invested in "perfection" that they refuse to connect with the real them behind the facade.

You know how you constantly refresh your Twitter feed, hoping for more likes on a funny tweet, but never really feeling satisfied with the number of likes? Yup, that's the exhausting cycle of prioritizing perception over authenticity, and it's how the narcissist lives through each day.

When you're asked to describe a narcissist, you might think of someone who spends way too much time talking about their career achievements or never seems to doubt themselves. But being narcissistic is more complex than that.

Contrary to popular belief, narcissism isn't a surplus of self-esteem. Rather, it is an insatiable thirst for admiration or appreciation, a need to be the center of attention and a belief in superiority over others. Unsurprisingly, narcissism can be damaging to familial, romantic, and professional relationships.

If there's someone in your life exhibiting an overinflated sense of self-importance, an excessive need for attention and admiration, a lack of empathy, and an expectation of special treatment reflecting a perceived superior status, you might have encountered a highly narcissistic individual. In seeing themselves as being of special status, this person naturally sees everyone else as beneath them.

The narcissist's excessive need for external validation and admiration is to compensate for their deep-seated feelings of inadequacy and validate the inflated sense of self. It's why they use manipulation tactics to maintain the facade of grandiosity and control over their victims. But despite this outward projection of charisma and confidence, they are extremely insecure and strongly afraid of abandonment and rejection.

This need for praise and admiration initially makes the narcissist seem charming and charismatic. These two qualities can quickly ignite a passionate romance with an empath. However, the narcissist's lack of empathy prevents them from understanding the empath's inner world and building a long-term relationship that is satisfying for both parties.

Pathological narcissism, commonly referred to as Narcissistic Personality Disorder, is different from regular narcissism, and I'll explain how when we discuss the spectrum of narcissism. According to researchers, this trait is normally distributed in the human population, with only one percent at the worse end of the spectrum.

The Narcissistic Personality Inventory (NPI) is the most common tool for measuring narcissism. Scores on the NPI range from 0 to 40, with the average score somewhere between mid-teens and low.

Healthy individuals with a high score may appear excessively charming, particularly on first meetings, but eventually expose themselves as vain. Such individuals tend to have stressful or awkward interpersonal interactions but form fundamentally healthy relationships.

Meanwhile, narcissism becomes pathological when it impairs an individual's daily functioning, leading to friction in relationships. Narcissistic Personality Disorder also manifests as antagonistic behavior stemming from attention-seeking and grandiosity.

It is arguably possible for people with pathological narcissism to truly fall in love and establish a mutually beneficial partnership. Instead, they seek to set stringent rules in romantic relationships and try to isolate their partners from loved ones, among other equally disturbing behaviors.

Keeping in mind the objective of this chapter, which is to help you further understand narcissists, and why they behave the way they do, we will now explore the narcissistic spectrum. The goal is to help you determine where on the spectrum the narcissist in your life falls and how to deal with that.

Narcissism and Its Spectrum

From a psychological perspective, narcissism is a trait we all possess in varying degrees. Like all traits, it exists on a continuum, and we all fall somewhere on that spectrum. In fact, a healthy amount of narcissism is necessary to live a satisfying life. Studies show that it increases confidence, ambition, and resilience.

But of course, any personality trait that falls on the extreme of its spectrum can become dysfunctional and pathological. As previously explained, someone with excessive narcissism has Narcissistic Personality Disorder, which can be officially diagnosed as a mental disorder.

A regular person with mild to moderate narcissistic traits may exhibit patterns of self-centeredness sometimes. But for pathological narcissists, it is a pervasive and deeply ingrained pattern of behavior.

There's a critical difference between someone with pathological narcissism or Narcissistic Personality Disorder (NPD) and someone with high degrees of narcissistic traits. Thanks to the recent rise in the popularity of narcissism, there's also an increasing interest in self-diagnosing the seemingly problematic people we know at home and work.

Though NPD is rare (it affects one in every 100 people), it appears like everyone thinks they know one or more narcissists – especially at work, where there can be a lot of friction and conflict. But for an individual to be diagnosed with NPD, narcissistic traits must interfere with functioning and manifest in various contexts. They must also negatively affect the person's identity and ability to establish and sustain healthy relationships.

A true narcissist's attitudes and behaviors are rigid and pervasive, with zero motivation to change. People with NPD usually don't recognize their behaviors as problematic. Conversely, someone with mild to moderate narcissistic traits is more likely to be conscious of their tendencies and open to seeking help.

When you view narcissism as on a continuum from mild to more severe narcissistic traits, you have different types of narcissism that fall somewhere along the spectrum. Here are the five types of narcissists on the spectrum:

1. Overt narcissist

The overt narcissist is the "classic" type that we're all familiar with. They are vain, boastful, outgoing, entitled, overbearing, competitive, and excessively preoccupied with how others perceive them. We also call this type other names, such as grandiose narcissist and agentic narcissist.

An individual with overt narcissism focuses on wealth, status, flattery, and power due to inflated self-importance and an overwhelming sense of entitlement. They are high-achieving, and tend to overestimate their intelligence, abilities, and skills. They are less likely to deal with unpleasant emotions like loneliness, sadness, or worry. That means they tend to feel good about themselves in general. At the same time, overt narcissists are highly sensitive to criticism, perceived or real.

2. Covert narcissist

Also called the vulnerable or closet narcissist, the covert narcissist isn't as recognizable as the overt narcissist. Like their counterparts on the extreme of the narcissistic spectrum, covert narcissists have an exaggerated sense of self-importance and thirst for attention and admiration. However, they display these behaviors more subtly and passively.

For example, where the overt narcissist boasts about their accomplishments and demands respect from people, the covert narcissist uses blaming, shaming, emotional neglect, and manipulation to make themselves the center of attention and get what they want. They tend to view and present themselves as a victim.

Covert narcissists also struggle with introversion, low self-esteem and confidence, defensiveness, and a propensity for shame, anxiety, and depression. They also experience a deep fear of not being enough, which they mask by playing the victim.

Just like overt narcissists, they are sensitive to criticism. But unlike overt narcissism, they tend to internalize criticism or take it more personally than intended.

Research suggests that both overt and covert narcissism aren't mutually exclusive. A narcissistic individual may display overt traits sometimes and covert traits at other times.

3. Antagonistic narcissist

An antagonistic narcissist is characterized by competitiveness, rivalry, and arrogance. While all narcissists are overly focused on perception, antagonistic narcissists take this to the extreme. They are obsessed with coming out "on top" in every situation. They don't mind exploiting others to get ahead in life. An antagonistic narcissist will start arguments and put people down without a second, though, all in a bid to gain the upper hand and come off as dominant.

Common behavior patterns include a tendency to take advantage of people and compete with them. Antagonistic narcissists are also disagreeable and prone to arguments.

Experts say that this is a subtype of overt narcissism and that antagonistic narcissists are less likely to forgive and forget than other types of narcissists. They also have major trust issues.

4. Communal narcissist

Now, this one is a subtype of covert narcissism. It is considered the opposite of antagonistic narcissism. Communal narcissists view themselves as altruistic and fair. However, research shows us there's a wide gap between their beliefs and behaviors.

Like a covert narcissist, a communal narcissist doesn't appear to be ego-driven or self-centered on the outside. You may perceive them as selfless. However, a communal narcissist's internal motivation is to be praised and admired, not help people.

To that end, you may find individuals with communal narcissism at the forefront of communities and social causes, often as the face of such movements. These people see themselves as caring, selfless, and empathetic and exhibit a pattern of moral outrage.

5. Malignant narcissist

As you know now, narcissism exists at different levels of extremity. Unfortunately, malignant narcissism is the most severe form. It causes problems for people with the condition. A malignant narcissist has many common narcissistic traits, like grandiosity and an inflated sense of self-importance. But along with that, they also tend to be vindictive, aggressive, sadistic, and paranoid. Malignant narcissists may share traits with individuals who have antisocial personality disorder. This creates a propensity for legal trouble and substance abuse.

Despite existing on the same spectrum, not all people with pathological narcissism look, act, and behave the same way. For example, one pathological narcissist might be a charming, well-dressed overachiever who has crafted a specific image to attract and draw people in. Meanwhile, another pathological narcissist could be an underachiever with a nasty sense of entitlement and a tendency to set low expectations for themselves.

These five types of narcissism – overt, covert, antagonistic, communal, and malignant – can all affect how an individual views themselves and interacts with others. In terms of treating NPD, this can be tricky because pathological narcissists don't feel the need to change. They see nothing wrong with behavior.

That is why you, as an empath, shouldn't concern yourself with trying to fix or rescue a narcissist. They don't need or want your help!

Exploring the Narcissist's Core Motivation

One thing I have realized from speaking to different victims of narcissistic abuse is that they find it hard to understand or accept that the narcissist's behavior has nothing to do with other people. It genuinely is all about the narcissist.

Of course, I understand why this simple concept may be difficult to grasp. It's natural to think that the motive has everything to do with you when someone behaves in a way that harms you specifically. This isn't true for narcissistic behavior, though. Despite what you may think, the narcissist isn't trying to damage or destroy you because you don't matter. You don't even exist or register with them. This is an internal war with themselves; you're just someone caught in the crossfire.

Now, I'm not saying that your being a victim is entirely accidental. That's not the case. But you aren't the motive. Nothing about you makes you the motive. You could be anyone. The narcissist's motive is self-preservation, and the battle is with themselves.

Initially, it seems like narcissists play games with others. When you examine it closer, you see that the game is really with themselves. You're just a tool they use to make themselves feel good. Everyone else is a prop in the narcissist's one-man show.

Many people struggle to understand this, perhaps because they can't grasp that degree of self-absorption. They find it hard to understand how someone could be so deeply and exclusively self-involved that others aren't even considered people. If you aren't narcissistic, it makes sense that you can't emotionally understand this.

Sure, you may understand it on an intellectual level and be able to put it in words. But emotionally? It'll likely always remain a mystery to us non-narcissistic folks. We just don't get it. How is it possible that the motivation for narcissistic behavior isn't to hurt another person? The answer lies in deconstructing the very idea.

First, you must realize that you're viewing the motivation through your eyes as the narcissist's victim. So, that makes it a personal perspective, no matter what. Of course, you're entitled to this perspective because being hurt by the narcissist is personal to you. It isn't personal to the narcissist, though. Not the way you think it is, anyway.

Why does the average human want to hurt others? Usually, because they've hurt us. At the same time, we have sadistic people who get off on inflicting pain. While both seem to align with the narcissist's motive, neither does.

You haven't done anything to hurt the narcissist, and they know this deep inside. You're merely a representative of their self-hatred and failure, a stand-in. The hurt comes from within. But the narcissist feels good projecting that hurt onto others because that relieves their pressure.

Some people go around with a punching bag, not because hurting the bag makes them feel good. They do it because it's an excellent way to blow off steam. This is the same thing with narcissists and their victims.

You must understand that narcissists don't see people the way normal functioning humans see people. As a normal functioning human, people are individuals with feelings, desires, needs, dreams, motivations, aspirations, and goals…. The narcissist doesn't see or care about any of this. From that alone, you can tell how empty their perception of others is.

To a narcissist, a person is only as valuable as how they can be used to make the narcissist feel. In other words, you're one-dimensional with one purpose only. Nothing else matters about you. Plus, they don't even realize anything about you as authentic. If you somehow force them to recognize a need or feeling that you have, the narcissist has zero interest in understanding it. The only thing narcissists have an interest in is the feelings you have about them. You're a mirror they look into for a good reflection of themselves.

Finally, you must understand that as long as all of these points are true, the narcissist's behavior doesn't register as abuse in their mind. And when you think of how the narcissist's dysfunction is structured, you realize this wouldn't have mattered anyway.

Narcissists are constantly fighting an internal battle. Therefore, from their perspective, they can only be victims, not abusers. What you know as abuse, they see as "blowing off steam." That tells us quite a lot. "Abuse" is the acknowledged, deliberate hurting of others. "Blowing off steam" doesn't acknowledge the other person at all. Instead, it centers on the narcissist's feelings and problems. And that's valid since it's how the narcissist views things.

Can you abuse a punching bag? No. So, the narcissist has no motive to hurt and destroy you because, as far as they see it, you are an object. The narcissist's core motivation is self-preservation.

We find narcissistic behavior shocking and callous, but from their perspective, it's nothing odd or terrible. This is how it works. Only the narcissist's problems are real. Only the narcissist's feelings are real. Only the narcissist is a real person.

Now, I want to be clear: this isn't to excuse the narcissist's behavior or rule it as not abuse. It is, in fact, abuse. There's no excuse, no justification. It doesn't matter what their motivation is because the result is the same: they're manipulative, self-involved, and utterly abusive.

Understanding the narcissist's motivations and behaviors helps you realize and accept that the problem isn't with you but with the narcissist. This makes it easier to let go of the hurt and resentment so that you can truly heal and move on to a happier, more fulfilling life.

Recognizing Red Flags: Common Narcissistic Tactics and Traits

Do you remember I said the narcissist's greatest weapon is their ability to make you turn against yourself? At the beginning of any relationship with a narcissist, they convince you they're anything but narcissistic.

Caring, attentive, and supportive, the narcissist grooms you by establishing trust before blindsiding you with hurtful behavior. Naturally, the transgressions seem unlike them, which baffles you. To avoid friction and drama, you tag it as an isolated event and try to forget about it.

In doing so, you overlook the very first red flag and the narcissist's first manipulation tactic: doubting the validity of your feelings and accepting the narcissist's perception of the situation as more factual or credible.

Knowing the narcissist, they repeat similar behaviors over the next few months, hurting then invalidating your feelings. Day by day, you start thinking your emotions and perspectives on issues can't be trusted.

If you decide to stand up for yourself, that can be problematic. After a selfish or hurtful act, the narcissist will deny doing anything wrong and shift the blame onto you. They will distort the situation and make themselves the victim and you the transgressor. Any attempts at defending and explaining yourself will be twisted to make you feel like "Chun Li, the bad guy." This is called gaslighting, and it's one of the narcissist's favorite manipulation tactics.

Being gaslit can be frustrating and infuriating. It may push you to lose your temper due to feeling "out of control," which only reinforces the feelings of shame and self-doubt that stem from the gaslighting. This is one way the narcissist attacks and deconstructs your belief systems.

Often, narcissists are attracted to partners with high emotional intelligence. As an empath, you're emotionally intelligent, self-aware, reflective, and attuned to others. But as the relationship progresses, a narcissistic partner instinctively realizes you have something they don't. Due to the absence of self-awareness and lack of affective empathy, they feel threatened because you possess something they don't understand.

The problem is that when narcissists feel small, they compensate by acting big. They seize control in relationships by devaluing you and acting superior. A narcissistic partner might say, "You're too emotional," "You're too sensitive," "You're soft," or "You think too much." They do this to further attack your sense of self. They belittle your most cherished and sophisticated gifts, leading you to view them as character flaws instead.

As this is happening, the narcissist also pretends to care about you in specific ways. You may see this as caring, but the objective is maintaining control. For example, suppose your car is faulty. In that case, the narcissist might offer to repair it to help you save money. Yet, they might take their sweet time fixing the car, resulting in you depending on them for transportation.

Narcissists can create a similar dynamic with your support system. A narcissistic partner may try to become friends with the people in your inner circle. They then use these people to throw you under the bus, obtain more control, and align your friends with themselves. This is a targeted infiltration of your life, and as it happens, the narcissist works hard to unravel your life. This is another tactic they use to attack and damage the very core of your being.

Grooming you, manipulating you into questioning your feelings and needs, inducing shame regarding your best qualities, and making you dependent on them are some of the tactics the narcissist uses to slowly destroy you from the inside out.

You must learn to recognize these sneaky attempts so that you can know when you're being targeted by a narcissist and quickly escape before your self-esteem takes a massive hit.

Here's something you must know about narcissists: They communicate differently than everyone else. They use their words as tools and weapons for manipulation to disguise their true intent. More often than not, there are red flags in conversations with a narcissist.

Given that, you must learn to see the motivations and true meanings behind anything the narcissist in your life tells you. It is crucial for your survival.

I'll make this easier by sharing examples of the narcissist's preferred language in communication. I'll also translate each example to illuminate the likely intent, motivation, and thinking behind it.

These are examples of what a narcissist might say if they were being unvarnishedly truthful about their objectives. They may or may not know their underlying motives, but in no world do they want you to know them.

- **"You're upset but I have nothing to do with that."** You're putting me on the defensive. I know you're upset, but that's your fault, not mine. I will never accept the blame or admit that I'm wrong. Nor will I apologize. That's for weaklings.
- **"You're too sensitive."** Your emotions are a problem. I don't know how to handle them, and I'm not interested in understanding why you feel this way. The only thing I can do is shame you so that you can stop bothering me with these pesky feelings.
- **"You're wrong."** I have no idea about the merit or credibility of what you're saying. But I must make you doubt yourself so that I can influence and control you in any way I want.
- **"I have never been more sure in my life."** Whatever I say at the moment, I believe it. I don't care if it's true or consistent with other things I have said in the past as long as I achieve my aim of silencing you. You're less likely to doubt me if I act sure of myself. Being challenged undermines me. I can't accept that, so I will undermine you in even worse ways.
- **"Stop trying to analyze me."** Everything you're saying about me makes me uncomfortable because they are true. Introspection terrifies me. Only talk to me if you have great things to say. Great things only!
- **"I never said that."** I know I said that, but I don't like how it makes me sound. You're not allowed to taint the self-image I have carefully constructed. I'll stonewall to confuse and

overwhelm you. Convincing you that I'm right is easy if I speak with absolute certainty.
- **"You've said this a million times."** No matter how often you say it, I won't listen. Good luck trying to get me to change through your silly complaints. I couldn't care less about the impact my actions have on you.
- **"You're too demanding."** Why do you have needs? Your needs are bothersome. You're meant to fulfill my needs, not the other way around.
- **"Stop being so selfish."** I am the only one allowed to be selfish. Don't you dare try to be me!
- **"You can trust me."** If you trust me, you'd be making the mistake of your life. But I must get you to believe it so I can continue to take advantage of you. Plus, saying this makes me feel good about myself.

Do not take a narcissist's words literally, or you'll find yourself constantly feeling confused and exhausted. The reality is narcissists mean the opposite of anything they say. They are deeply afraid of being perceived as "weak," "inferior," or "flawed." Everything they say is an attempt at masking their insecurities.

For instance, to avoid appearing like a loser, the narcissist presents themselves as the best. To avoid appearing ignorant, they project absolute certainty. To avoid feeling empty, they act larger than life.

To help you recognize red flags, I'll end this chapter by sharing common signs to watch out for to determine whether your friend, partner, family member, etc., is a narcissist.

- **Excessive need for admiration:** They constantly seek validation and praise from others, often fishing for compliments or expecting special treatment.
- **Lack of empathy:** They find it challenging to understand or care about other people's feelings or perspectives. They may dismiss or minimize your emotions and prioritize their own needs above yours.
- *   **Sense of entitlement:** They believe they inherently deserve special treatment or privileges and may become upset or angry if you don't give them what they want.

- **Manipulative behavior:** They may use charm, flattery, or manipulation to get their way. They can be skilled at gaslighting or making you doubt your perceptions and experiences.
- **Grandiosity:** They have an inflated sense of self-importance and may exaggerate their achievements, talents, or abilities. They often expect to be recognized as superior with or without commensurate achievements.
- **Difficulty with criticism:** They may react defensively or aggressively to any criticism or perceived slight, viewing it as a personal attack on their self-esteem.
- **Lack of accountability:** They rarely take responsibility for their actions or mistakes, instead blaming others or making excuses.
- **Shallow relationships:** They may have numerous superficial relationships but lack deep, meaningful connections with others. They may use people as tools for their gratification rather than valuing them for who they are.
- **Exploitative behavior:** They may exploit others for their gain, whether financial, emotional, or otherwise, without regard for the well-being of others.
- **Patterns of control:** They may try to control or manipulate you in various aspects of your life, such as who you spend time with, what you do, or how you feel.

It's important to note that having one or two of these traits doesn't necessarily mean someone is a narcissist. However, notice a pattern of several of these behaviors over time. It may be worth considering whether the person exhibits narcissistic tendencies and whether the relationship is healthy for you.

Being an empath, one of the best strategies to protect yourself in general and against a narcissist is boundary-setting.

That's why the next chapter is all about helping you master the art of setting effective boundaries. We will discuss the importance of boundary-setting, the best techniques to utilize, and how to deal with boundary violations from a narcissist and other people looking to drain you of your energy.

Time to find out how you can start protecting yourself!

CHAPTER FOUR:
The Art Of Setting Healthy Boundaries

Imagine yourself at your favorite artist's concert – Taylor Swift, maybe. The music is booming, Taylor is on stage, and the atmosphere is electrifying. But there's another concert-goer in front of you, and this person keeps bumping into you – even spilling their drink while yelling along to the songs off-key.

Personal boundaries are like the security at the concert. They are there to make sure you can enjoy the music and performance without anyone getting in your face or ruining your fun. That way, you can cheer, sing along, and connect with those around you, without crossing the line of what's acceptable.

This concert represents your life, energy, and time. Taylor Swift and her music represent your passions and goals. The crowd at the concert is the people in your life—friends, family, coworkers, neighbors, acquaintances, etc.

Not all boundaries are effective. Some are like nonexistent security – people invade your personal space, you get trampled on, and it feels like you're at Travis Scott's Astroworld concert. Meanwhile, other boundaries are rigid. It's like being stuck at the back of the concert where you can hear the music but can't enjoy the experience.

Without proper boundaries, as an empath, you may find yourself frequently overwhelmed by the unending influx of emotions and energy from other people. You might also feel drained, anxious, or lost, as people feel when surrounded by a chaotic concert crowd.

Now, think about the friendly but firm security guard at the concert. They direct you to a good spot, politely step in when someone oversteps, and do their best to control the concert so everyone can have a great time. Similarly, proper boundaries help you regulate emotional energy flow, ensuring that you go through life without getting overwhelmed by others' emotions.

With them in place, you can connect and form meaningful relationships while maintaining your sense of self and protecting your well-being. You're in control of your experience but still part of the fun.

If you don't set boundaries, you may find yourself either taking on too much of other people's emotional energies, like when you get trampled at a concert with lax security, or withdrawing completely to preserve your energy, akin to being stuck at the back of the concert – unable to fully attune to the experience.

Establishing healthy personal boundaries enables you to handle social interactions and interpersonal relationships in a way that safeguards your emotional well-being and helps you thrive.

Boundaries can be negotiated. Security at the concert might allow a friend to move closer during your favorite songs. Similarly, you can relax your boundaries for close relationships or special occasions.

Furthermore, boundaries shouldn't be rigid. They can change at any point. The ideal security level at a concert depends on the type, such as a mosh pit vs. a classical recital. Just like personal boundaries, they may need to be adjusted over time in new situations.

We don't set healthy boundaries to be selfish. Instead, we set them to create a space where we can thrive and enjoy the concert (life) to the fullest. Setting firm boundaries is all about controlling your environment and the atmosphere while still participating with the vibrant crowd.

Usually, people learn about boundaries during childhood, but this is rarely the case with empaths and narcissists.

For empaths, their nature makes it hard to limit what they can and can't tolerate. You feel responsible for others' feelings and needs, so you tend to take on burdens that aren't yours. This manifests as:

- Difficulty saying no
- People-pleasing tendencies
- Feeling drained by others' emotions

This can result in exhaustion and resentment.

In contrast, narcissists disregard other people's boundaries because they have an inflated sense of self-importance and lack empathy. This manifests as:

- Disregarding others' needs and feelings
- Manipulation and control
- Needing constant admiration

This difference in how they handle boundaries can create conflict, especially in relationships between empaths and narcissists.

We'll start this chapter by delving into the importance of boundaries for you as an empath. Then, I will share the most effective techniques for setting and enforcing healthy boundaries with the people in your life. Finally, you will learn how to deal with repeat boundary violations, especially from narcissists.

Get ready to become a boundary-setting pro at the end of this chapter!

Importance of Boundaries for Empaths

Your phone rings. It's a friend who always calls you to vent about something wrong in their life. You don't want to pick up the call because speaking to them drains you, but you do, cringing hard, pick up the phone.

Or you're at the local grocery store when a random stranger comes up and starts narrating their life's entire story to you. Yes, you're in a hurry, but you stay and listen to them. What if they have no one else to talk to?

It's your child's basketball game, and you're there to cheer her on as always. Someone comes up and asks if you'd be willing to join a school volunteer group. Even though you're already a member of at least ten other committees and groups, you accept because you don't want to disappoint them. After all, you want to support your child anyhow you can.

These situations would have been a terrific opportunity to set a boundary. Yet, you can't seem to do that because it feels incredibly hard. The average person has a default sense of boundaries: "This is me and I'm a separate entity from everything else." But an empath doesn't have this. Instead, you have a highly refined antenna that never fails to pick up on people's feelings, needs, desires, and pains. So, you must be extra intentional about stepping back from others.

You need good boundaries to instill a sense of self and separation from everyone around you. Since you soak up everything around you, I understand how difficult it can be to put your foot down and say "NO."

As an empath, you need healthy boundaries because:

- Others' feelings, needs, and experiences aren't yours to absorb or prioritize.
- It's crucial that you feel safe and grounded within your body.
- You find it easy to give to others, but giving to yourself is just as important to preserve your energy reserves.
- Taking on other people's emotions and energies always adds emotional baggage to work through.

Being an empath makes you liable to enable bad behaviors and habits in others. Enabling is dysfunctional for you and the other person.

A friend recently emailed me: "I enjoy taking an evening walk around my neighborhood for my mental health. Lately, I've had my friendly neighbor invite herself along. She waits for me to come outside, then joins me. She's a nice and friendly woman who enjoys my company. But my evening walks are the only alone time I get each day. How do I get her to stop coming along without appearing mean?"

Now, I understand where my friend is coming from. She's an empath, and like most empaths, she thinks it's selfish to put herself first. This is one of the most common objections empaths seem to have toward boundaries: setting them feels selfish, cold, and punitive like they're building a sturdy wall between themselves and others. However, boundaries aren't like walls; they are fences. And a good fence makes for a good neighbor.

Boundaries let people who care about you love and support you in ways you want and prefer. They establish clear limits on what you consider acceptable or harmful, ensuring people don't have to read your mind.

With boundaries, you can engage in interpersonal relationships openly and fully, knowing you've drawn clear lines on your limits and made it easier for anyone in your life to respect your needs. It is impossible to have a healthy relationship without boundaries.

Sure, my friend liked her neighbor and wanted a good relationship. If she couldn't stop the neighbor from crashing her evening walks, she would become resentful and angry. Eventually, she would have lashed out because she felt frustrated. Thus, setting a boundary here would be vital for preserving their relationship, enabling my friend to care for her neighbor without decentering her own needs.

I asked my friend how many evenings she was open to spending with her neighbor – from Sunday to every evening of the week. She said that she wouldn't mind walking with her once a week on Saturdays.

So, I sent a script she could forward to the neighbor the next day: "Hey there! I'm going to resume walking by myself again during the week. It's the only alone time I have every day, and it's really important for my mental health. Would you mind joining me on Saturday evenings when I am more rested and relaxed?" Her neighbor loved the suggestion, and it worked out for both parties.

It's normal to wonder if setting boundaries makes you mean, but it doesn't. When you draw clear lines in your relationship, you're being kind to yourself and others. Yes, it'll feel uncomfortable. That happens with conflict generally—if you ask for a medium-well burger and it's rare, you might choose to eat it instead of complaining.

Boundary-setting feels uncomfortable because when you set a boundary, you're pointing out something you don't like in another person's behavior (and communicating a limit that isn't established yet. More importantly, you're asking the other person to adjust for the good of your relationship.

Empath and all, that probably made you throw up a bit in your mouth. You aren't alone in this. From experience, people have difficulty setting boundaries because they don't feel comfortable with it. I feel that way, too. I don't always find it easy to decline a friend's request for financial help, say no to a coworker, or ask my partner for some alone time.

Asking for what you need, advocating for yourself, and speaking up at the moment can feel uncomfortable. However, internalizing the belief that other people's feelings and needs are of more value than yours is both uncomfortable and harmful. Unfortunately, it's what you do every time you don't set a much-needed boundary to avoid conflict.

Realistically, there's no comfortable solution to people overstepping your limits. However, you've got two options: one causes short-term discomfort and leads to significant long-term benefits, whereas the other creates an endless cycle of pain that leaves you feeling resentful, anxious, angry, and unworthy.

Which do you prefer?

And if you have any relationship with a pathological narcissist, you're probably stuck with the latter option…for now.

It's time to choose the other option—one that will lead to improved self-esteem and confidence, better health, more time and energy for the things that truly matter, and more fulfilling connections.

Setting boundaries may feel uncomfortable, but I bet it will be worth every effort.

So, how do you start setting those much-needed personal boundaries – especially with narcissists and other toxic people?

Effective Techniques for Setting Clear and Firm Boundaries with Narcissists

Before I show you how to set clear and firm boundaries with narcissists and other people, here's a breakdown of what a boundary is and what it isn't:

- **A line in the sand:** Think of a boundary as a clear line demarcating your and someone else's space. It tells the person what you are and isn't comfortable with, what you

will and won't tolerate, and how much you're willing to give in a personal or professional relationship. It can range anywhere from physical touch to how much you share to how you spend your time.
- **Respectful:** Boundary-setting is about stating your limits to others in a firm but respectful manner. It shows others how to interact with you and what they expect from the relationship.
- **Essential for healthy relationships:** Boundaries make you feel safe, valued, and respected, ensuring your needs are fulfilled. Setting boundaries also allows others to establish their own limits.

What a boundary isn't:

- **An iron wall:** As I stated before, a boundary isn't a wall that helps to isolate yourself and completely shut others out. Rather, it's a fence that enables you to safeguard your physical, mental, and emotional well-being while building healthy connections that last.
- **A weapon:** Setting boundaries isn't about controlling or punishing other people. It's about caring for yourself and improving your overall health. When you set a boundary, you put yourself first and create a space where you and others feel comfortable.
- **Static and unchanging:** Boundaries can also evolve as situations and relationships develop over time. After all, it's natural for your needs and expectations to shift. You must adjust your boundaries accordingly to match up with your current circumstances.

Now that you know what boundaries are and what they aren't, the question is: How do you set firm, healthy boundaries?

Here are some of the most effective techniques for empaths:

- **Know what you want.**

What matters to you in personal and professional relationships? What doesn't matter? What drains you of energy? What do you find acceptable and unacceptable? Answering these questions is the first step to setting clear and firm boundaries with everyone else.

Whether platonic or romantic, you can't get your needs met in a relationship if you don't identify them. A good way to know what you need is to reflect on your beliefs and values.

Ask yourself:

- What traits do I want in a friend or romantic partner?
- What behaviors do I consider unacceptable?
- What qualities do I love in others?
- How do I like spending my time?
- What gives me a sense of fulfillment?
- What material things matter to me and why?

Using these as prompts, write down a list of your non-negotiables – things you absolutely won't tolerate in an interaction. It could be anything ranging from not being yelled at to respecting your time.

The more understanding you have of yourself, the easier it'll be to imagine the boundaries you need. If independence is important, you will want to set boundaries around your finances with a partner. If you value privacy, you might set a boundary with that coworker who likes to lounge around your workspace.

Also, assessing how you feel about others can help in this process. It can help identify crucial boundaries. After any interaction with someone in your life, you can reflect on how you feel using the prompts below:

- Did the person make comments or "jokes" that made you feel a way you don't like?
- Did they do something that made you feel uncomfortable or unsafe?
- Did you feel pressed to do things that didn't align with your values or beliefs?
- Did the person's requests and expectations overwhelm you?
- Did it feel like they were imposing on your autonomy or sense of control?

Take a moment to reflect on these questions. They'll help you determine where you need to set limits with the other person in the future.

- **Communicate your needs and boundaries**

Effective communication is pivotal in establishing and maintaining boundaries. Expressing your needs to others the right way can make all the difference. Poor wording, vague requests, and ambiguous or rushed conversations can make it difficult for others to understand and respect your newly established boundaries.

First of all, timing is everything when telling people about your boundaries. The best time is when you and the other party feel relaxed and focused on each other. Do not try to talk to them about it during an argument or conflict. You're better off waiting for things to calm down and then circle back.

Naturally, you will feel nervous – it's not something you can help. In that case, you should write down what you intend to discuss so that you can rehearse speaking assertively about your needs and limits.

It's also vital that you use the right delivery. Narcissists love pushing other people's boundaries to test how much we'll let them get away with. Therefore, you mustn't be afraid to tell them "NO" or "I need some space." Don't be scared to convey your feelings and needs with "I" statements. It's a powerful communication technique because it lets you express yourself without appearing accusatory or defensive. For example, say, "I feel overwhelmed when you raise your voice" instead of "You always raise your voice at me."

- **Do not JADE**

JADE is an acronym for Justify, Argue, Defend, or Explain. If there's something we've made clear, it's that narcissists are master manipulators. Any explanation you give while setting a boundary will automatically become a weapon fashioned against you. The narcissistic individual will use it to twist everything in their favor.

The best way to handle any objection or rebuttal is to calmly repeat the boundary. For example, if the narcissist says, "That doesn't even mean anything. You're just too sensitive," reply with, "I understand you may disagree, but I will end the conversation if you raise your voice at me."

Instead of explaining yourself or arguing why your boundary is necessary, focus on establishing consequences. Let the other person know the outcome of crossing the drawn line. Make sure the consequence is something you're willing and able to follow through on. Do not back down at the last minute.

For example, "If you talk to me like that again, I'll end the conversation and take a break for the rest of the day." Then, when the narcissist violates your boundary, calmly but firmly follow through with the promised consequence.

Narcissists are skilled at obtaining personal information to manipulate and control others. Be very intentional about what you share, particularly in the early stage of your relationship.

As you set and enforce boundaries with the narcissist in your life, take the following steps to protect yourself.

- **Minimize emotional reactions.** The narcissist thrives on drama and chaos. Emotional responses are nothing but ammunition. You mustn't give them the satisfaction. They'll try to bait you with harsh words and criticism. When that happens, take a few deep breaths and excuse yourself from the conversation.
- **Practice self-care.** To support your emotional and mental health, try activities that make you feel alive and full of energy. Consider spending time in nature, hanging out with loved ones, or doing things you genuinely enjoy.
- **Consider limited contact or no contact.** Sometimes, drawing lines in the sand just isn't enough. In that case, the healthiest alternative is to distance yourself from the narcissist completely. You might need this if they're a family member, such as a parent or married partner. Going no contact is harder than it sounds, but you come first.
- **Ground yourself.** Grounding techniques can help you build a protective shield around yourself, protecting your energy and managing your emotions. Meditation or visualization exercises can also be helpful. They can help you center yourself and detach from the emotional mess a narcissist might be creating.

- **Build a support system.** Surround yourself with people who are positive, and supportive and respect your boundaries. A strong support network of friends, family members, or even a therapist can offer a safe space to process your experiences and receive encouragement.

Establishing boundaries with a narcissist can prove to be particularly challenging, especially for empaths. So, be patient with yourself, focus on your well-being, and don't be afraid to seek additional support. The most important thing is to protect yourself and create a safe space to thrive.

Throughout the rest of this book, we will shed more light on the protection strategies I briefly shared in this chapter. To make boundary-setting incredibly easy for you, though, let's look at a visualization exercise for setting and enforcing boundaries with people who drain your emotions and energy.

Boundary-Setting Visualization Exercise for Empaths

This guided visualization is an excellent exercise for helping you identify and strengthen your personal boundaries, particularly when interacting with others who drain your energy.

Instructions:
- Find a quiet, comfortable space where you won't be interrupted.
- Close your eyes and take a few slow, deep breaths.
- Imagine yourself feeling relaxed and centered.

Now, follow these steps for visualization:
- **See yourself:** Picture yourself standing in a beautiful meadow. Feel the soft grass beneath your feet and the warm sun on your skin.
- **The energy bubble:** Imagine a shimmering bubble of light surrounding you. This bubble represents your personal, energetic space.

- **Notice the colors:** Observe the color of your bubble. Is it clear and vibrant, or dull and cloudy? The color reflects the strength and permeability of your boundaries.
1. **Healthy interactions**: Visualize healthy interactions within your bubble. See supportive people who energize you and respect your space. Their presence brightens your bubble.
2. **Unhealthy interactions**: Imagine someone who drains your energy approaching your bubble. Notice how their presence affects the bubble. Does it shrink or dim?
3. **Strengthening your bubble**: Imagine taking a deep breath and infusing your bubble with white light. See it becoming stronger and more resilient.
4. **Setting boundaries**: Practice saying "no" to the energy drain in a firm but kind voice. See your bubble repelling any negativity they try to project.
5. **Healthy detachment**: Visualize yourself calmly detaching from the energy drain, perhaps gently guiding them away from your bubble.
6. **Refill your energy**: See yourself absorbing the positive energy from the meadow, refilling and revitalizing your bubble.

Once you're done, slowly bring your awareness back to your body. Wiggle your fingers and toes if you'd like. Take a few moments to integrate the visualization. How do you feel now? Whenever you feel drained by someone, recall this image of your strong, vibrant bubble.

Keep in mind that this is just a starting point. Practice this visualization regularly to strengthen your boundaries and become more confident in protecting your energy.

Dealing with Repeat Boundary Violations

One sad thing about life is that people who are manipulative, controlling, and narcissistic tend to be repeat boundary violators. This also applies to those with a poor sense of self, who aren't necessarily narcissists.

Along the line, you'll find that determining what to do with people who repeatedly violate your boundaries can be quite challenging. There's no definitive answer to "How do I deal with people who constantly violate my boundaries?" But I'll give you some insights to help you arrive at a perfect answer.

First, you must consider a few variables:

- **Who's violating your boundaries?** The nature of your relationship, power differential, and intimacy are critical here. How you handle a violation from your mother will differ from how you respond to your coworker or boss, and even that will be different from how you deal with a neighbor.
- **Is the person open to change?** Are they willing to work on improving your relationship? Are they sensitive to your feelings and needs? Would they be willing to try counseling with you?
- **How long have they been doing this?** Understandably, it'll be much harder to change long-term behavioral patterns. Still, this might be possible if the person is truly willing (which you probably shouldn't expect from a narcissist).
- **Are you setting boundaries the way you should?** From experience, many people overestimate their boundary-setting skills. Sure, there will be times when you back down, feel overwhelmed or tired, and don't feel like following through with enforcing the boundaries. Unfortunately, boundaries are ineffective if you only enforce them sometimes. You must be firm and consistent, especially when dealing with a narcissist or someone who doesn't respect you. Such an individual will look for holes in your rules and use them against you. Therefore, you must be assertive and follow through with consequences.

I don't say this to make you feel bad about yourself if you aren't consistent with boundaries and consequences. Many people encounter the same problem. But I want you to know what you can control (mostly yourself). Self-awareness is crucial; it empowers us.

If you can tell when and where you're slipping up, being accountable and compassionate toward yourself becomes easier.

Now, back to the original subject of what to do with people who repeatedly violate the boundaries you set.

- **Record the violations**. Write down every breach and your response. That way, you can look for weak spots and address them. If you notice you aren't being clear and firm, adjust that. Seeing the pattern will help you decide if the violations are things you can tolerate.
- **Use the Broken Record technique**. If someone repeatedly ignores your boundaries, calmly and firmly repeat your message. Don't get emotional or engage in a debate.
- **Set consequences with follow-through**. Don't make empty threats. Decide on consequences for boundary violations and stick to them. This could be walking away from a conversation, limiting contact for a period, or even ending the relationship.
- **Investment vs. ROI.** Consider how much effort you're willing to put into this relationship. Is the other person open to working on respecting your boundaries? Are they showing any effort to change?
- **Consider emotional distancing.** In some cases, detachment or ending the relationship might be the healthiest option. Know that you can't control someone else's behavior, but you can control how much you expose yourself to negativity.

Here are practical examples of how to deal with boundary violations:

Craft a quick, polite script to address the violation.

- **Example:** Someone is constantly venting negative emotions to you. Script: "I hear you're going through a tough time. However, when you vent to me constantly, it starts to affect my mood. Can we talk about something else, or would you prefer to talk to someone else about this?"

Use nonverbal cues to create distance.

- **Example:** A friend gets uncomfortably close during conversations. Step back or gently place your hand on your armrest as they lean in.

Broken Record: Repeat your message, but offer solutions.

- **Example:** A family member keeps asking for money despite you saying no. Broken Record with a twist: "I can't lend you money right now. However, I'd be happy to help you create a budget to get back on track financially."

End the interaction when a boundary is crossed.

- **Example:** A coworker gossips constantly. Time-Out: "Excuse me, I need to use the restroom." (Take a break and return when ready to resume the conversation on your terms.)

Follow through with an action if the violation continues.

- **Example:** A roommate doesn't clean up after themselves. Consequence: "I've repeatedly asked you to clean up your mess. Since it continues, I won't be cleaning up after you anymore.

Keep the following in mind when you try the above tips:

- Be clear and concise. Do not sugarcoat your message.
- Stay calm and respectful. Do not get emotional or escalate the situation.
- Focus on the behavior, not the person.
- Practice with a trusted friend before using these in a real situation.

Remember, you can only control your actions and no one else's. Be kind to yourself. Setting boundaries is an ongoing journey, not a destination. There will be bumps along the road. Prioritize self-care and surround yourself with positive people.

Your empathy can only thrive in a space with healthy and firm boundaries. Don't be afraid to embrace the art of setting strong personal boundaries starting now.

As an empath, you feel all the feels, but how do you keep them from feeling you? The next chapter will explore emotional self-defense so you can start shielding your energy the way you should!

CHAPTER FIVE:
Emotional Self-Defense: Shielding Your Energy

During a recent meeting, a client, Susan, known for her radiant positivity and empathetic nature, showed signs of feeling distressed and burnt out. I could tell she felt overwhelmed because her usual demeanor wasn't there.

Naturally, I asked about her well-being. She confided in me that she was feeling generally negative. In her words, it was like "an emotional contagion." I suspected it was a case of empathic overload and told her as such. It was a common problem for empaths and other highly sensitive people. So, I talked to her about the importance of learning emotional self-defense techniques, especially as an empath.

Do you know how healthcare professionals wear protective gear to prevent contamination? Well, empaths use certain protective strategies to shield themselves emotionally. These encompass mindfulness practices and visualization exercises to protect themselves in emotionally charged situations.

Do you remember the concert analogy I shared in the previous chapter? Think of energy-shielding techniques as taking a step back from the speakers. You can still hear the music perfectly, feel the vibrant energy of the crowd, and sing along to Taylor enthusiastically. But there's little emotional overload. You can enjoy the concert without getting overwhelmed. It's like wearing mental earplugs that filter out the useless background noise and only let in the sounds that matter. It allows you to savor the pure joy of the concert and the experience. That way, you can be present and grounded without your energy getting hijacked by the roaring crowd.

When I say energy shielding, I'm talking about creating a barrier around yourself to protect your energy from being sucked and drained by vampires or ensure you don't get overwhelmed by other people's negative emotions and energies. Energy shielding techniques are excellent emotional self-defense tools for empaths.

Common energy shielding techniques, which I'll show you how to use, include:

- **Visualization**: This technique involves conceiving a protective barrier around yourself using imagination. The barrier could be a bubble of light, a mirror reflecting negative energies away from you, or your sacred space.
- **Grounding**: This helps connect your energy to Mother Earth. Picture roots underneath your feet, anchoring you to the ground so nothing can move or affect you.
- **Carrying protective objects**: Many empaths carry crystals and other spiritual items to provide security and drive away negativity.

The concept of empaths and energy shielding isn't yet scientifically proven. But the techniques I'll share in this chapter can be incredibly helpful for people such as yourself who feel overwhelmed and drained by others' emotions and energies.

As you utilize these techniques, it's just as important to cultivate discernment and better manage your sensitivity instead of fully blocking out all emotions. Remember, you're meant to feel…so feel.

Ultimately, combining energy-shielding techniques and regular ways of protecting yourself emotionally is best.

In that light, let's look at how you can emotionally distance yourself in interactions with the narcissist or anyone else who drains you of energy.

Practicing Emotional Distancing in Interactions with Narcissists

Emotional distancing involves disconnecting or disengaging from others' emotions. This may happen because you're unwilling or unable to connect with others. Sometimes, people practice emotional distancing in response to a stressful or challenging situation. Other times, it stems from an underlying psychological problem.

As an empath, emotional distancing can make a significant difference when used purposefully to disengage from specific people or groups. It can help you detach on a healthy level from those who demand too much of your emotions and energy.

When dealing with a narcissist, emotional distancing may be voluntary. You can choose to be emotionally removed from them or the relationship, especially if the narcissist is a friend or family member.

It helps to be proactive about removing yourself from emotional situations. This is an option if you have a coworker or family member who upsets or drains you greatly. You can be deliberate about not engaging with them. Doing so will help you remain calm during your interactions.

In this case, emotional distancing is a protective measure to prepare yourself for any situation that may evoke an intense emotional response.

Before we talk about how to detach during interactions with a narcissist, first, we'll look at how to do this in general. Remember that emotional distancing is about creating space between your emotions and your reactions, not shutting down your feelings entirely.

- **Take a break**. Anytime you feel overwhelmed, take a break from the situation. You can try a walk, deep breathing, or whatever helps you calm down. For example, if you're disagreeing with a friend, you could tell them, "Hey, this is getting heated. I would like to take a break and come back to it later."
- **Mindful observation**. Don't let your emotions sweep you away. Instead, observe it curiously. Label the emotion and where the feeling is in your body. Think about why you might be having that emotion. For instance, suppose your heart is racing. In that case, you might acknowledge, "I'm feeling angry right now and it's making my chest tights. This is because I feel unheard."

- **Journaling**. To process them better, write down your thoughts and emotions. Doing this will also help you gain more perspective on people, things, situations, etc., that trigger your emotions the most. You might notice how you've handled similar situations when you reread entries. Journaling is a great technique for better understanding your feelings and those of others.

All interactions with a narcissist can spiral into chaos and drama. Their emotional outbursts and manipulative behavior can be draining, leaving you overwhelmed and holding on for dear life. But with the multi-pronged approach, I am about to share, you can successfully detach during an interaction with a narcissistic mother, father, sibling, friend, boss, or romantic partner. Doing so can prevent your interactions from escalating into something you can't handle.

Here are my best tips for detaching in the moment:

- **Become a broken record**. As you know, narcissists welcome drama and emotional reactions as ammunition. Counter this penchant for negativity by repeating a calm, neutral statement – like a broken record – when you don't want to budge on something. Doing so forces the narcissist to acknowledge what you're saying.
  - **Example**: Your narcissistic parent lashes out, "You never listen to me!" Respond calmly, "I hear you, but I must take some space to think about this on my own." If they insist, calmly repeat the same statement. Do not justify or explain yourself. Just keep repeating the statement until they get the message.
- **Try the fog technique**. Do not give in to the narcissist's attempts at manipulating your feelings. Acknowledge their feelings, but don't accept responsibility for them. Doing this takes away the strength of their accusations, disarming them.
  - **Example**: They start guilt-tripping you, "This is all your fault!" Respond with, "I understand you're upset but I won't be addressed that way. We can

revisit this conversation when we can both be calm and constructive about it."
- **Subtly shift the focus**. When the narcissist tries to bring up something negative during a conversation, gently steer them in an entirely different direction. Choose a neutral topic that they can't manipulate.
  - ➢ **Example**: They attempt to attack you with comparisons, such as, "Why can't you be more successful like your cousin?" Casually reply, "Speaking of success, did you see that article about [neutral topic]?" Note that this tactic only works if it's appropriate for the situation.

Nonverbal cues like body language and facial expressions are just as important in creating distance during interactions with a narcissist or another toxic personality type. Here are some tips.

- **Create physical space**: Physical distance is very powerful in communicating detachment. If you're sitting, gently scoot back in your seat. And if standing, take a step back to draw a clear line between you.
- **Use eye contact**: You may be unable to break eye contact completely because that would be considered rude or dismissive. But you must avoid intense staring so you don't appear threatening. That ensures the situation doesn't escalate.
- **Cross your arms**: Crossed arms are a universal sign of distance. It's great for setting a physical boundary during your conversation. It says, "I'm not open to drama and negativity!"

During the interaction, you may find it hard to repeat a calming mantra in your head. This is an excellent way to anchor oneself and protect against emotional hijacking. Repeat phrases like, "Stay calm," or "This doesn't define me." When emotions start to rise, take slow, deep breaths. This activates your body's relaxation response and helps you regain control.

Now, you must remember that the aim is to disengage, so do not get sucked into an argument for any reason. Remember, JADE, don't even bother wasting your energy engaging someone who thrives on manipulating others' emotions.

Though these strategies are effective, they're merely short-term solutions. They can help you detach temporarily at the moment, but you still need long-term options. For instance, can you limit or go no contact? Or perhaps end the relationship? If those are the best options for your well-being, that's exactly what you must do.

Planning before an interaction with a narcissist always makes a difference. You can make a pre-arranged phone call, excuse yourself to the restroom, or have a close friend ready to rescue you if necessary. An escape routine enables you to end the meeting promptly before it snowballs out of control.

Next, look at the best shielding exercises for protecting and cleansing your energy.

Energy Shielding: Exercises for Grounding and Protection

Being highly sensitive to others' emotions makes you so vulnerable that you need practice and patience to master keeping other people's feelings out. And that's where energy shielding comes in.

Empaths are vulnerable to sensory information in the environment, which makes them prone to overstimulation and overload. Like introverts, they need downtime and time away from others' negative energies to recharge and restore.

However, it is possible to stop sensory overload in its tracks before it can even get you down. You can even choose which emotions to process and which you don't want to.

When someone brimming with negative energy walks into a room where you are, you immediately pick up on the negativity. You lose grip on your previous feelings, letting it all go to absorb the energy of the negatively charged individual. This is exhausting.

"All it takes is a phone call," my friend used to say. Only one phone call could wreck her mood and possibly affect her whole day or week.—until she learned how to shield herself with grounding and visualization exercises.

Energy shielding will help you and the people in your life. The question is, how do you practice shielding?

As I explained earlier, it involves creating a barrier between yourself and everything else. Positive things, such as compliments, good intentions, jokes, etc., can get through the protective barrier. But negative things like harsh criticism, rude comments, ridicule, verbal attacks, and anything that affects your self-esteem badly can't get through. Instead, they hit the barrier, drop down, and disappear.

Deflecting negative energy with shielding means not accepting it. It lets you stay firm in your preferred emotional state. Nobody can turn your optimism to pessimism. After shielding, if a narcissist walks up to you and tries to stir something, the barrier immediately activates and sets a boundary.

I'll share three different exercises for practicing energy shielding to protect yourself.

Exercise 1: Guided Protection for Empaths

This exercise combines visualization and breathwork to help you feel centered and protected. It can be done anywhere you feel comfortable, but ideally in a quiet space.

Instructions:

- Find a comfortable seated position. You can choose to sit either in a chair with your feet flat on the floor or cross-legged on the ground.
- Shut your eyes and take a few deep breaths. Inhale slowly through your nose, sensing your belly expand, and exhale completely through your mouth.
- Imagine a beam of white light descending from above, enveloping your entire body. Feel this light cleansing and purifying your energy field.
- Visualize roots growing down from your base chakra (the area at the base of your spine) and going deep into the earth. See these roots connecting you to the stability and grounding energy of the planet.

1. Imagine the earth itself radiating a warm, golden light. Feel this light rising through your roots, filling your body with security and strength.
- At the crown of your head, visualize a sparkling white shield forming. This shield protects you from any unwanted or draining energies.
- As you continue to visualize, begin slow, rhythmic breathing. Inhale for a count of four, feeling your grounding connection strengthen. Breathe out gradually for six counts, releasing any tension or negativity.
- Imagine drawing in more of the earth's grounding energy with each inhale. With each exhale, see any unwanted energy flowing away through your roots and dissolving into the earth.
- Continue for several minutes or as long as you feel comfortable. When you feel ready, softly redirect your attention to your body and wiggle your fingers and toes.
2. Take a few deep breaths and slowly open your eyes.

You can repeat this exercise as often as you need throughout the day, especially in overwhelming situations. If you find it difficult to visualize, focus on the sensation of your breath and the feeling of your feet on the ground. You can even add affirmations to your practice. Repeat phrases like "I am safe" or "I am protected" silently while visualizing the shield.

The key is finding a practice that helps you feel centered, protected, and connected to your inner strength.

Exercise 2: Sensory Grounding Meditation

This grounding exercise utilizes movement and sensory details to help you stay rooted in your physical presence. Find a quiet space where you can move freely for a few minutes.

How to practice:

1. Stand tall with your feet positioned about hip-width apart and take several deep breaths. Feel the ground beneath your bare feet (or socks, if necessary). Wiggle your toes and notice the sensations.

2. Slowly shift your weight from side to side, feeling the connection between your body and the earth with each movement.
3. Now, bring your awareness to your sense of smell. Take a deep inhale through your nose and identify three distinct environmental scents. It could be fresh air, coffee brewing, or even a faint cleaning product.
4. Next, focus on your sense of touch. Rub your hands together, feeling the warmth and texture of your skin. Notice any jewelry you might be wearing, the coolness of a breeze, or the fabric of your clothing.
5. Look around the space and identify five objects of different colors. Name each color silently to yourself, focusing on the vibrancy and detail.
6. Finally, bring your awareness back to your breath. Take a few slow breaths, feeling your belly go up and down each time you breathe in and out.
7. Stand quietly for a moment, integrating the sensations you've experienced.
8. Gently shake your body and wiggle your fingers and toes to release residual tension.

You can repeat this exercise anywhere you feel overwhelmed or disconnected. If you can't remove your shoes, focus on the feeling of the floor beneath your feet. For an added challenge, close your eyes during parts of the exercise and rely solely on your other senses.

This practice brings awareness to your physical body and surroundings, helping you feel anchored in the present moment and less susceptible to outside energies.

Exercise 3: Anchoring with Crystal Visualization

This exercise combines visualization, breathwork, and the power of intention to create a powerful anchor within you. When you connect to the earth's core and your inner strength, you can find peace and stability even in challenging situations.

Instructions:

1. Find a peaceful place where you can sit comfortably for a few minutes. You can sit in a chair with your feet flat on the floor or cross-legged on the ground.
2. Remove your shoes and socks to connect more deeply with the earth's energy, if possible.
3. Shut your eyes and take a few deep breaths. Inhale slowly through your nose, sensing your belly inflate like a balloon filling up. Hold briefly, then breathe out fully through your mouth, releasing tension with each exhale.
4. Now, visualize a smoky quartz crystal positioned at the base of your spine, where your root chakra resides. Smoky quartz is valued for its grounding qualities, and its smoky color symbolizes its link to the earth. Visualize the coolness and smooth texture of the crystal in your mind's eye.
5. Picture the crystal pulsing with a soft, gray light. As it pulses, tendrils of light extend downward, like thick, healthy roots. These roots extend deep into the earth, traversing layers of soil and rock, until they reach a vibrant network of glowing red energy—the core of the planet.
6. Feel the earth's warmth radiating up these roots, infusing your smoky quartz crystal with stability and security. Imagine the core's red energy mingling with the crystal's smoky gray light, creating a grounding force within you.
7. With each inhale, visualize the red energy traveling up the roots and filling your crystal. Feel your core becoming more grounded and secure.
8. As you exhale, feel any negativity or unwanted energy leaving your crystal and traveling down the roots, dissolving harmlessly back into the earth's core.
9. Pay attention to your body's physical sensations. Feel the weight of your body pressing down on the chair or floor. Notice the coolness of the air or the sun's warmth on your skin. These sensations further anchor you to the present moment.
10. Continue for 5-10 minutes or as long as feels comfortable. When you feel ready, softly redirect your focus to your body and wiggle your toes and fingers.
11. Take a few deep breaths and slowly open your eyes, feeling centered and grounded.

If you don't have smoky quartz, visualize another crystal that resonates with you for grounding, such as black tourmaline or hematite. To enhance the experience, you can also play calming music with natural sounds in the background. Repeat this exercise daily, especially when feeling overwhelmed or disconnected.

Now, let's look at how to avoid emotional drains by energy vampires.

Recognizing and Avoiding Energy Vampires

How often do you feel sapped of life after talking to a friend, family member, neighbor, or coworker? Perhaps you feel anxious, irritable, or sad after spending time in their company. If you have people in your life who constantly feed on your attention, care, and emotions, we call them energy vampires. They leave you stressed, exhausted, and overwhelmed. So, it's time to learn how to avoid getting drained emotionally.

There are different reasons why people could be knowingly or unknowingly draining your emotional energy, including personality disorders, mental health conditions, trauma, and attachment types. That's why you must know how to recognize the toxic people in your life.

Knowing who will drain your energy on the first meeting is hard. But after several instances of being around them, you can watch out for patterns of feeling:

- overstimulated
- apathetic
- irritable
- annoyed
- stressed
- fatigued

Often, these people come across as friendly and needing your help. Naturally, you feel inclined to help them, but when the drain starts it can lead to a breakdown. They thrive on negativity, constantly complain about their lives, gossip excessively, and fixate on their problems without seeking solutions.

Every interaction with energy vampires leaves you feeling depleted or wiped out. Pay attention to a pattern of feeling this way after being in the company of certain people.

Different kinds of energy vampires might be sapping your energy:

- **The victim**: The only thing some people know how to do is victimize themselves. Their victim card is always ready to go. Think of that one person who always has a new sob story about something that happened to them, real or imagined. Everyone else in the world is against them while they're innocent. Individuals like this often complain about how much they hate their lives.
- **The negative thinker**: Do you know anyone who always sees the glass as half empty instead of half full? Yes, that's the type – individuals with a negative attitude toward everything and everyone. They aren't necessarily malicious, but negative thoughts and feelings rule their interactions. While it's normal to vent sometimes, these people make that their default mode. They fixate on problems, criticize others, and never see the silver lining, even if you shove it in their face.
- **The critic**: These people's only job is to invest their time and energy into criticizing people, things, situations, etc. They find fault with everything, and nothing is ever good enough.
- **The takers, not givers**: Every interaction feels one-sided. They monopolize your conversations with what's happening in their lives but never show any interest in yours. Reciprocity is one of the key elements of genuine emotional connection. If you have such a person who constantly makes you feel like a sounding board without being supportive, be wary of them.
- **The blamer**: They don't ever take responsibility for anything. All they do is point the finger at other people, always ready to hand out bundles of shame and guilt. This can be emotionally taxing because it creates an environment

where you feel compelled to accept responsibility for their situations.
- **The dramatizer**: Some people not only attract drama; they create it. You'll always find them amid a catastrophe or crisis that requires your help and support.

You can identify the energy vampires in your life by watching out for the following traits:

- Needing to be the center of attention at all times.
- A tendency to exaggerate every little thing.
- Playing the blame game in every situation.
- Feeling worn out after talking to them.
- Constantly taking from you without ever giving back.

Now, here's how to protect yourself from energy vampires, regardless of the category:

- **Adjust your expectations**

This is the most crucial step, informing how you follow the remaining tips. If you're close to the energy vampire, it's natural to feel disappointed and upset when they don't reciprocate your support. Therefore, it's best to adjust your expectations and accept that they will never show up for you. See them for who they are, and taking necessary self-protection steps will be easier.

- **Master the art of making excuses**

Always having a polite excuse handy can help avoid interactions with energy vampires. For example, you might say, "I wish I could chat more, but I have a different commitment coming up," or "Wow, that sure sounds like stress. Can we talk more about it when I have sufficient free time?"

- **Limit your exposure**

Whether setting boundaries or using shielding strategies, you can limit your exposure to energy vampires as much as possible. For example, if they're a coworker, you have no choice but to work with them. Still, you can avoid getting coffee or going on a lunch break together.

- **Use social media wisely**

Sometimes, you meet energy vampires online instead of in real life. But the good news is that it's easier to curate what you see on social media platforms to limit exposure to toxicity. Mute, unfollow, or block anyone who peddles negativity or drama.

- **Get busy**

It's OK to be busy! I know this goes against your nature as an empath, but you shouldn't feel pressured to always make yourself available. If an energy vampire asks to hang out, gently reschedule to when you have overflowing energy or suggest an activity that won't require much emotional investment. Go for a walk, grab a coffee, or do something that allows for lighter interaction.

Sometimes, you may not be able to fully avoid these people. When that happens, ensure you set limits for conversations. For instance, suggest a phone call with a specific time limit or ask to catch up over coffee instead of having dinner.

Know this: You don't have to explain yourself to anyone. Energy vampires shouldn't get an explanation for why you're taking steps to protect your energy from them. A simple "NO" or "I need some alone time" is perfect.

With the tips shared throughout this chapter, you now have the basics to build a toolkit of techniques to handle interactions with emotionally draining people. It doesn't stop you from being empathetic and supportive. But having this toolkit means you can now practice emotional self-defense against toxic people like a narcissist.

It's much harder to navigate relationships with a pathological narcissist when they're a family member, sibling, friend, etc. The next chapter will take you on a journey to maneuvering narcissism in different kinds of relationships.

Get ready!

CHAPTER SIX:
The Narcissist In Your Life: Handling Different Relationships

The way you approach narcissism will depend on the kind of relationship you have with the narcissist in your life. The strategies are the same whether it's a personal or professional relationship. However, dynamics dictate how you apply these strategies in your life.

Be it a romantic partner, parent, sibling, friend, boss, or coworker, narcissists are all the same. They also wreck similar levels of havoc in your life. However, this may be influenced by how long you've known the narcissistic individual.

This chapter explores how different relationship dynamics influence narcissistic behavior and how to navigate each dynamic correctly. You'll also learn how to cultivate healthy, interdependent relationships and avoid dysfunctional ones in the future.

First, let's discuss the factors influencing the empath-narcissist dynamic in different relationships.

Narcissism Manifestation in Different Relationships

The following are factors that influence how narcissism manifests in personal and professional relationships:

Power Dynamics

Some relationships, like parent-child or boss-employee, have an innate power imbalance. Narcissists can exploit this for control, making it harder to challenge their behavior or set boundaries.

Children rely on their parents for love, care, support, and guidance by default. Narcissistic parents can take advantage of this dependence to twist their kids' sense of self and emotional well-being.

In the workplace, there's a structural hierarchy that gives the boss more power than the employee. This unequal power can make challenging your narcissistic boss feel impossible, making you feel helpless and leading to increased stress.

Meanwhile, romantic relationships and friendships usually have a more balanced dynamic. But being who they are, the narcissist uses manipulation tactics and emotional abuse to tilt this dynamic in their favor.

Emotional Intimacy

Relationships that have more intense and deeper emotional connections, like close family members and romantic partners, offer a fertile dynamic for narcissistic behavior. The narcissist can exploit affection, trust, and a sense of obligation for abuse and control.

Romantic relationships thrive on emotional intimacy and vulnerability. The narcissist can use manipulation tactics to exploit your trust and affection. This impact is often particularly damaging since it affects more intense feelings.

In terms of family, the bonds are typically deeply ingrained and complicated. A narcissistic mother or father might control you with fear, obligation, and guilt (FOG). This can make it harder to establish boundaries and emotional distance.

Conversely, more superficial relationships, like casual acquaintances, evoke less intense emotions. By extension, they offer less room for manipulation. Still, the narcissist can engage in self-promotion and use you to fulfill certain needs. Being an empath makes this even easier.

- **Frequency of Interactions**

There are some people you have to interact with daily, such as a narcissistic partner or coworker. The need for control and validation can create a toxic environment at home or work. You can limit interactions with an extended family member, but you may not be able to do that with a husband, wife, mother, father, supervisor, or work colleague.

- **Expectations of Reciprocity**

Healthy friendships and romantic relationships thrive on give-and-take. The narcissist disrupts this dynamic because they make you feel inferior and undervalued. They prioritize their needs and neglect yours, leading to a one-sided and emotionally unfulfilling relationship.

There's a basic expectation of unconditional love and affection in familial relationships. Unfortunately, a narcissistic parent's love and support is conditional. They weaponize the basic expectation of parental care to control their child.

It's important to understand these factors. That way, you can recognize how narcissism might manifest in your specific relationships. Using that awareness, you can take the right approach to dealing with the narcissist in your life, whether that's a controlling friend, guilt-tripping parent, or demanding boss.

Now, we'll discuss how to navigate each dynamic, starting with family.

Navigating Family Dynamics with a Narcissist

Dysfunctional families come in varying forms, among which we have the narcissistic family. By this, I mean a family with at least one narcissistic parent or grandparent. In such a dynamic, everyone has a specified role they dare not venture out of. The structure and roles are established to enable narcissists to fulfill their needs while everyone else's needs are ignored.

Also, blaming, gaslighting, FOG, emotional blackmail, and disrespect are some of the most common tactics used in narcissistic families to further the abusive person's control.

The structure of a narcissistic family dynamic usually includes the following:

- **The narcissist** – rules over everyone else in a reign of terror.
- **The enabler** – reinforces the narcissist's power by helping to facilitate the abuse of other family members.
- **The golden child** – is treated as the "superior" child and molded after the narcissist's idea of perfection.

- **The scapegoat** – held responsible for everything that goes wrong in the family.

Image trumps all in this family. The narcissistic parent is obsessed with presenting the illusion of a "perfect family." They need this to project their desired image to the world. All problems and misfortunes are blamed on the scapegoat, whereas the narcissist takes credit for everything that goes right. All family members must stick to their assigned "role," or they risk evoking narcissistic rage.

Sure, the narcissist in your life is family, and you love them despite their flaws. It's natural to feel obligated to stick around. Or you might not want to upset the family dynamic.

To make your decision, answer these questions:

- How do I genuinely feel around this person?
- Is it possible to limit our interactions?
- How can I strengthen my boundaries with them?
- Can I maintain the relationship, or will it hurt too much to cut them off?

In many cases, limiting contact is the best option. Start by reducing how often you see them or reach out to them. You may have to cut off all ties if that doesn't work.

Limiting contact with a narcissistic family member may look like this:

- Establishing time limits on conversations
- Only hanging around them in the presence of other people
- Not borrowing their money unless they pack back for the last time.

If these don't work, no contact might be your next step.

Going "no contact" is the favorable option if this familial relationship is damaging different aspects of your life. If you believe your physical, mental, or emotional well-being is at risk, I suggest discontinuing contact abruptly without informing the individual.

- Change phone number and email address
- Unfollow and block them on all social media platforms

- Inform others and ask them not to share private information with the narcissist

You'll feel lost and sad when you limit or cut off all contact. But remind yourself that you tried to make it work.

Writing them a final letter (that you don't send) can help facilitate closure and begin the healing and recovery process.

Dealing with Narcissistic Friends

Most people practice making friends from infancy. Many made their first friends as toddlers. There are different ways to make friends—at work, through daily or weekly activities, and sometimes through neighbors. Those who are lucky still have people they've known since childhood in their lives. These friendships have stood the test of time.

As noted earlier, healthy friendships are built on give-and-take. Some friends are seasonal (college), some are here for a reason (common experience), and others are there for the rest of your life. In other words, not every friend is here forever.

Everyone that comes into your life teaches you a vital lesson. Friends like the narcissist teach you that not everyone is a true friend because some people are just that self-absorbed.

Being friends with a pathological narcissist requires discounting your own nature, i.e., the you that should be. Think about this: Why are you friends with a highly narcissistic person? What are the costs and benefits of this relationship? Why do you think you aren't allowed to have feelings and needs and, therefore, be willing to sacrifice them?

You're the most important person you need a relationship with. By being friends with a narcissist, you're bruising your sense of self. So, how do you deal with that?

First, write down the pros and cons of having this narcissistic person as your friend. Then, take a step back and objectively evaluate yourself. Write down the things you like and dislike about yourself. Record your hobbies, passions, interests, and choices you'd like to make for your future. Use these to create boundaries that value and honor the person you're meant to be.

Next, think about the time, emotions, and energy you put into making the narcissistic friend happy and validated. Then, make a conscious decision to invest these things into making yourself happy. Be deliberate about your happiness.

Remember that the narcissist will never be happy or satisfied, no matter what you do for them. And that regardless of how much you invest, the relationship will always be one-sided and parasitic. You really can't change that.

When something great happens to you, the narcissistic friend will neither be happy nor supportive. They have a nasty competitive spirit, with little attention to share. Buy a new dress, car, or house, and they'll feel like you're taking something that belongs to them.

If you make plans with friends outside of your circle without them, the narcissistic friend will feel jealous and excluded. The belief is that you take something away from them when you get things for yourself.

If you decide to maintain a friendship with a narcissist, follow the boundary-setting guidelines I provided. That's the only way to protect your sense of self and identity. It's how you maintain your power and become who you're meant to be.

Coping with a Narcissist at Work (Boss or Colleague)

The workplace is one of the hardest places to manage toxic personalities. But it gets even worse when the toxic person is a narcissistic boss or coworker. You can avoid and manage narcissism in other relationship dynamics. This is rarely the case in professional settings, though.

I know from experience that working with a narcissist can be frustrating and exhausting. So, it's important to find wiggle room to protect yourself, no matter how small.

We've all had that one difficult coworker, and most people have had their fair share of disagreements and conflicts in the workplace. However, being difficult isn't the same as narcissism.

A narcissistic boss or coworker may:

- steal credit for other people's work.
- avoid accountability for mistakes.
- spread malicious lies about other coworkers.
- react defensively to feedback.
- take shortcuts and do unethical things.

Now, when the narcissist at your workplace is a superior, that's a different ball game. A narcissistic boss can make a nightmare of your dream job. Having such a boss can make you fearful of sharing new ideas and displaying creativity or throwing you under the bus.

Meanwhile, the job market is quite congested. So, even the mere idea of getting a new job can induce anxiety. Perhaps your only option is to "make the best" of coping with your narcissistic boss – or you like your job and wouldn't like to leave on account of them.

How you cope with a narcissistic boss or coworker depends on the circumstance, but you can do it. The best way to avoid your boss' or coworker's behavior negatively impacting you is to remove yourself from the toxic environment. But if that's not an option, the following tactics can help protect your emotional and mental health/.

- **Set boundaries**. Firm boundaries are critical when dealing with a narcissist in the workplace. You must be assertive about your responsibilities, workload, and personal space. Establishing boundaries will help to maintain a much-needed sense of control, making it easier to protect your well-being. If you have a description of your responsibilities, review it to clarify what's expected of you. Also, research what constitutes workplace harassment in your state.
- **Avoid engaging.** There's no point in engaging narcissists. When your boss confronts you over anything, do not engage. Instead, redirect his attention to issues that have a direct impact on your work and well-being. Your boss might try to bait you into disagreements—walk away.

- **Document interactions**. Start recording all unpleasant interactions with your boss. Write down instances of positive feedback, criticism, and inappropriate behavior. Document the dates, times, people present, and direct quotes. Store this information on your personal device instead of your workplace computer.
- **Manage expectations**. Narcissists often set unrealistic expectations for others. Attempting to meet your boss' expectations will only cause stress and anxiety. If you meet one, they set another impossible expectation. It never ends. Let them know your capabilities by setting realistic goals and managing expectations. Remember that your boss might behave the same way even if management gets involved.
- **Build a professional network**. Do you know anyone who has had a similar experience with a narcissistic boss? How did they manage? How can you reach them now? It helps to lean into your professional network as you hone your skills. This will help you land a new job at a healthier workplace while making sure you're supported during the difficult phase of dealing with the narcissist.

As you navigate narcissism in the workplace, it's important to keep your guard up professionally and emotionally. I recommend steering clear of office "drama" and strengthening your boundaries while working on landing a new job.

When resigning, prepare for flattery, verbal attacks, or bargaining to get you to stay. Remember to stand on business and keep the resignation meeting brief. It's always a good thing to remind yourself in that moment that you'll never have to interact with the narcissist again.

Power of Interdependence: Cultivating Healthy, Fulfilling Relationships

Humans are wired for connection. Even people with an avoidant attachment style value connecting with others, especially in romantic relationships. You must connect to bond and become intimate with your partner. The long-term success of a relationship relies on the strength and quality of both parties' emotional connection. Having a foundation where your needs for trust, security, dependency, nurturance, guidance, and predictability are consistently met is also equally important.

To connect on this level, a relationship needs healthy dependence, also known as interdependence. This healthy dependence falls somewhere on a spectrum.

On one end, we have interdependence, where you and your partner depend on each other emotionally, have autonomy, and are vulnerable with each other. On the other end, we have unhealthy dependence, AKA codependency, where poor boundaries, enmeshment, loss of self-identity, and coercive control are the key components.

An empath-narcissist relationship is often codependent. By this, I mean people in the relationship lean on each other in an unhealthy way. The narcissist relies excessively on the empath at the expense of the latter's well-being. Plus, all sacrifices and benefits gained from a relationship go to the narcissist only.

Empaths need to "fix" others, thanks to their empathy and compassion. As you know, this is what attracts you to the narcissist in the first place. The belief then becomes a core part of your relationship with them.

The narcissist wants attention and admiration, which you readily provide. Your constant validation feeds their ego. Since you also struggle with setting and enforcing boundaries, the narcissist takes advantage of your good intentions and tendency to sacrifice yourself.

Ultimately, this creates a codependent dynamic in your relationship. Your identity becomes enmeshed in being a "fixer" as you lose your sense of self, trying to please the narcissist. But the narcissist can't be fixed, and they never feel fulfilled due to their disorder. The cycle continues for as long as you let them exploit and manipulate you.

Naturally, you don't want to jump from one codependent relationship to another. You must learn how to nurture interdependence in your relationships from now on. That way, you can stop falling victim to people looking to exploit your good nature.

Many confuse interdependence for independence, but they are two different things. Independence is about autonomy and self-reliance, whereas interdependence is about mutual reliance and interconnectedness between partners and people.

Interdependence means you and your partner have an independent life. You're two individuals who choose to be in a partnership together. You pursue your individual goals and have separate lives but rely on each other for support and happiness.

Here's how to build interdependence:

- **Be your own person**. Maintain your identity by maintaining your interests, hobbies, and friendships outside of your relationship. This keeps you interesting and makes your time with your partner more special.
- **Encourage open communication**: Express your needs, wants, and feelings without fear or hesitation. Listen attentively to your partner and see their perspective on issues. Ensure they do the same for you.
- **Respect each other boundaries**: If a new partner violates your boundaries at least two times, take that as an immediate red flag. In an interdependent relationship, both partners are entitled to "alone time" without guilt. Be deliberate about your boundaries.
- **Be a team**: Solve problems and make decisions that affect you. You're team members working toward a happy and successful relationship.

Interdependence is all about balance. Only seek relationships with strong individuals who support you and validate you.

If you've been in a relationship with a narcissist long enough that your sense of self-worth is affected, the next chapter is dedicated to your healing and recovery. There, I will show you how to start healing from narcissistic abuse.

Get ready for a step-by-step guide toward rebuilding your identity and self-esteem while healing from gaslighting and emotional manipulation.

CHAPTER SEVEN:
Healing And Recovering From Narcissistic Abuse

You finally understand why your abuser behaved the way they did and why you suffered as much as you did. It's a huge relief learning the reason for the cycle of abuse you endured. The disjointed pieces are coming together and they make sense as a whole. You've read everything available, listened to what you can, watched what there is to watch.

Now, you know as much as humanly possible about narcissism in relationship dynamics. You've educated yourself to the point where you could teach a master class if anyone asked. Unfortunately, this doesn't make you feel better. From a logical perspective, you should feel safe because you've ended the relationship – but you don't.

Leaving an abusive relationship with a narcissistic partner can be extremely challenging – yet the healing and recovery journey that comes after is probably more difficult and painful. Narcissistic abuse leaves you reeling with confusion, feeling drained, and questioning your perception of reality after months or years of emotional abuse.

Many survivors learn about narcissistic abuse and seek therapy, then turn on themselves when nothing seems to be working. They blame themselves and block self-compassion. This makes them feel frustrated and alone.

Even when you've identified patterns of narcissistic abuse and manipulation tactics in your relationship, you may not realize the depth of damage done to you. The subconscious mind is the showrunner, but you aren't aware of that. The shame, blame, guilt, anxiety, etc. feel normal to you. They're not your original thoughts, but you can't tell the difference.

The healing and recovery process typically involves reliving your trauma and painful memories. You may question past decisions or flirt with reigniting a dysfunctional relationship. Despite the toxicity, the dynamic feels overwhelmingly difficult to leave behind.

The most crucial step to begin this journey is understanding that you aren't at fault for staying or feeling entrapped in the dynamic. You must acknowledge that you were in a dysfunctional relationship with a partner who abused and exploited you. Labeling the abuse is the key to kick-starting your healing.

Of course, to heal, you must know what the relationship took from you. In other words, what are the emotional and psychological effects? It's impossible to address these without knowing what they are.

After discussing the impact, we will focus on how you can utilize self-compassion to rebuild your self-esteem and self-worth. Finally, you will learn how to heal from the gaslighting and emotional abuse you suffered for months or years.

Time to dig in!

The Emotional and Psychological Impact

The intensity and significance of a traumatic experience and related behavior are imprinted into the amygdala. This is the part of your brain where the "fight or flight" response is activated. The amygdala is inside the limbic system, located in your midbrain.

When you encounter a stressor, real or imagined, the brain releases adrenaline and cortisol – two stress hormones that imbue your body with a surge of energy so that you can fight the stressor or flee from it. We call this the acute stress response.

When you experience chronic stress, your mind instinctually tries to protect you by rationalizing, compartmentalizing, or outright denying the impact of your suffering. Similarly, traumatic events like narcissistic abuse hijack the logical part of your brain. This makes it difficult to derive meaning from the experience or think of it rationally. You're stuck in survival mode.

Many survivors rely on the prefrontal cortex—the part of the brain responsible for abstract thinking—to try to understand what has happened to them. Logical reasoning is a fundamental activity of cognition. In other words, they try to heal their trauma with rational thinking. This, of course, is impossible because we cannot think our way out of pain.

In the early stage following the abuse, you will endure a wave of challenging emotions. The abuse has poisoned you mentally and emotionally for a long time. Now, it's time to let everything out.

It's normal to swing between rage and utter numbness. Seemingly minor reminders may trigger a breakdown. You may also feel a sense of loss, grief, sorrow, and loneliness. Some survivors even have nightmares about traumatic memories.

Narcissistic abuse can have such damaging effects that you may feel profound confusion, causing you to doubt your perception of reality. You might reflexively make excuses for the narcissist's behavior or blame yourself for the abuse.

The trauma of narcissistic abuse can leave many scars on your emotional and mental health, such as:

- Anxiety: You may feel extremely anxious or fearful in new relationships. Some victims experience separation anxiety, which makes them feel disoriented and panicky when they aren't with their abusers. It's common to have anxiety and panic attacks or feel hypervigilant. The symptoms will let up over time.
- Depression: Many victims of narcissistic abuse feel depressed after leaving the dynamic. You may struggle with feelings of worthlessness after years of being gaslighted and manipulated.
- PTSD: As a survivor, you may experience post-traumatic stress disorder. Your brain will constantly be on the lookout for threats because you're stuck in "fight or flight." You feel like you must be on guard at all times. After all, you never know what your abuser might do next. The chronic hypervigilance can make it impossible to relax. You may avoid specific people, places, things, activities, or situations that serve as reminders of the abuse.

- Loss of identity and sense of self-worth: It's common for survivors to feel like they don't know themselves anymore. Gaslighting is a form of brainwashing. As such, it can diminish your sense of self and self-worth. You may no longer remember the person you were before the abuse. Many survivors also develop trust issues with others (especially in new romantic relationships). They also find it hard to make decisions alone. You might feel unable to decide on anything or get confused by the simplest decisions.
- Physical symptoms: The trauma from narcissistic abuse can also manifest physical symptoms, such as stomachaches, headaches, body aches, digestive issues, insomnia, and more. These symptoms often arise from the constant state of hypervigilance.

The good news is that full recovery is possible after the abuse. But it takes commitment, patience, and hard work to undo the harm. You may struggle with mood instability, poor boundaries, and low self-esteem for years unless you address these effects swiftly.

Self-compassion is the singular most important tool you need on this healing journey. You'll never be able to make a full recovery without it. Practicing self-compassion is the basis for setting boundaries, rebuilding identity and self-esteem, and achieving post-traumatic growth.

So, let's talk about embracing self-compassion to rebuild your sense of self and self-esteem.

Rebuilding Self-Esteem through Self-Compassion

Self-esteem is how you see yourself, good or bad. Self-compassion is treating yourself with kindness, empathy, and understanding, especially during hard times. After surviving narcissistic abuse, you will no doubt contend with feelings of worthlessness, insecurities, inadequacies, self-doubt, and low self-esteem. However, self-compassion can be your most powerful tool in rebuilding a healthier and more positive perception of yourself.

When I say "practice self-compassion," I mean treat yourself as kindly as you would treat a close friend in a similar situation. Accept that you're imperfect like everyone else; therefore, it's only normal to make mistakes.

During the healing phase, it's important to forgive yourself. But you can't do this without self-compassion. Forgiving yourself is a form of kindness. Forgiveness is vital for reclaiming your identity and well-being. It paves the way for your recovery.

Self-compassion means acknowledging and accepting everything you've been through. Don't deny or suppress – that will only make it worse. Instead, embrace the experience with gentle understanding.

After the abuse, there will be moments when you lose your temper... with yourself. You will blame and beat yourself up for letting it happen. Sometimes, you'll treat people harshly and then criticize yourself more harshly for doing that.

Normally, it's easy to be hard on yourself – most people do that much more than they realize. When you suffer as you have, though, it only amplifies how tough you are on yourself. But there's a better way to deal with this, and it's through self-compassion.

Here's why self-compassion is a powerful tool for rebuilding your self-esteem:

- **Nurtures self-acceptance**: Often, we source our self-esteem from external validation and achievements. This makes it shaky. With self-compassion, you learn to accept yourself, flaws and all. That establishes a strong foundation of inner self-worth that doesn't crumble in the face of adversity and setbacks.
- **Decreases self-criticism**: The aftermath of narcissistic abuse will have you tearing yourself down with negative self-talk. However, self-compassion will motivate you to treat yourself with kindness and understanding, like how you'd treat a loved one having a hard time.
- **Builds resilience**: Being kind to yourself equips you to face challenges and bounce back from them. It can facilitate healing and recovery, ensuring you don't get stuck in a negativity loop.

To practice self-compassion, you'll need self-awareness. Notice your internal dialogue, especially when thinking about the relationship. You might use self-critical language a lot in your self-talk. Then, you must respond to this with understanding and empathy. Finally, you must accept that we all make mistakes and experience adversity. You aren't alone.

This exercise is an excellent tool for practicing self-compassion every day.

Daily Self-Compassion Exercise

This exercise is designed to be done daily for a few minutes. Find a quiet, comfortable space where you won't be interrupted.

1. **Acknowledge and validate your emotions:**
   - Start by taking a few deep breaths and directing your focus to your body. Notice any physical sensations connected to your emotions – tightness in your chest, a knot in your stomach.
   - Gently name the emotions you're experiencing. It's OK if there are multiple emotions or if they feel confused. You might say, "I'm feeling hurt, angry, and confused right now." Allow yourself to experience these emotions fully, without any judgment.
2. **Acknowledge your common humanity:**

Remind yourself that experiencing pain and hardship is part of the human condition. You are not alone in feeling this way. Think about friends, family members, or even public figures who have spoken out about their struggles.

   - Silently repeat a mantra like, "Everyone experiences challenges in life," or "This pain is a normal response to an abnormal situation."
3. **Cultivate self-soothing through kindness:**
   - Imagine holding or cradling a younger version of yourself or someone you deeply care about who's hurting. This could be a childhood version or a metaphorical image.

- Visualize yourself offering them words of comfort and understanding. What would you say to this vulnerable person?
- Now, with the same tenderness, say those comforting words to yourself silently or aloud. Examples include, "You are strong and worthy. You will get through this," or "It's OK to feel sad and angry after what you've been through."

4. **Practice self-acceptance without shame:**
   - It's common to question your actions or decisions during an abusive relationship. Acknowledge that you may have made mistakes, but remember that everyone does. The narcissist's manipulation can be incredibly confusing and distort your perception.
   - Instead of dwelling on self-blame, offer yourself understanding. Say something supportive like, "It's OK that I didn't see the abuse at first," or "I did the best I could with the information I had at the time." Forgive yourself for trusting someone who ultimately betrayed that trust.

5. **Ground yourself in the present moment:**
   - After acknowledging your emotions, gently bring your awareness to the present moment. This helps move away from ruminating on negative thoughts or reliving painful experiences.
   - Pay attention to your breath. Feel the air as it enters and exits your nostrils, or notice the gentle rise and fall of your chest. Notice your physical sensations – the way you're sitting, the feel of your clothes on your skin. You can also focus on external sights or sounds in your environment.

6. **End with a Strength-Based Affirmation:**
   - Conclude the exercise with a positive affirmation about yourself and your future. This should be a personal statement that resonates with you. Examples include, "I am worthy of love and respect," "I am learning and growing from this experience," or "I am becoming stronger and more resilient every day."

Self-compassion is a skill that develops over time. Don't get discouraged if it feels awkward or forced at first. Acknowledge small improvements and remember that setbacks are a normal part of the process.

After the exercise, consider journaling for a few minutes about your thoughts and feelings. This practice can assist you in processing your experiences, recognizing areas for growth, and monitoring your progress over time.

Make self-care a priority. Nourish your body with healthy foods, get enough sleep, and engage in activities you enjoy – engaging in activities like spending time outdoors, listening to music, or connecting with loved ones. In the next chapter, you will learn more about self-care practices for empaths.

Finally, surround yourself with people who believe in you and offer genuine support. Think about joining a support group for survivors of narcissistic abuse or seeking therapy from a qualified professional specializing in trauma recovery.

Now, here's how you can incorporate kindness into your day-to-day:

Here's a list of ways to weave self-kindness into your daily routine:

Mornings:

- **Gentle Start**: Wake up a few minutes earlier to savor a cup of tea, stretch gently, or read a few pages of an inspiring book. Set a positive tone for the day.
- **Affirmation Power**: Write down a positive affirmation about yourself and repeat it as you prepare. "I am worthy of love and respect" or "I am strong and capable" are great starting points.

Throughout the day:

- **Body positivity**: Catch yourself criticizing your appearance. Instead, acknowledge a part of your body you appreciate or focus on the amazing things your body can do.
- **Nourish your body**: Pack healthy lunches or snacks to avoid eating unhealthy options when hunger strikes. Listen to your body's cues and take breaks when needed.
- **Digital detox**: Schedule breaks from social media and constant screen time. This allows you to focus on the present moment and connect with yourself.

- **Stay hydrated**: Carry a reusable water bottle with you and sip from it throughout the day. Staying hydrated can enhance both mood and energy levels.

Evenings:

- **Mindful movement**: Take a short walk, do some yoga stretches, or dance to your favorite music. Physical activity is a great stress reliever.
- **Gratitude**: Before bed, reflect on 3 things you're grateful for, big or small. This simple practice cultivates a positive outlook.
- **Creative outlet**: Spend 15-20 minutes on a creative hobby - drawing, writing, playing music - to express yourself and unwind.
- **Tech-free zone**: Power down electronic devices at least an hour before bed. This allows for better sleep and promotes relaxation.

Bonus tips:

- Schedule time each day for activities you genuinely find fun, whether reading a book, watching a funny show, or spending time in nature.
- Make time for friends and family who uplift and encourage you.
- Don't overload yourself. It's OK to decline requests that drain your energy.
- Everyone makes mistakes. Practice self-forgiveness and learn from them, but don't dwell on them.

During this healing process, always don't forget to treat yourself with the same kindness, patience, and understanding that you would offer to a dear friend facing a difficult time. You are worthy of love, respect, and a life free from abuse.

How to Heal from Gaslighting and Emotional Abuse

Gaslighting and emotional abuse warp your view of reality and leave you doubting your sanity. Healing from both means reclaiming your reality shattered by the narcissist, piece by piece.

Validation is the first step. This isn't about assigning blame but acknowledging the facts of your experience. You weren't crazy. The narcissist subjected you to a targeted assault on your perception of reality. Journaling can be a great tool for validating yourself. Don't fixate on the abuse. Write down the events as they occurred to strengthen your truth and counter the abuser's narrative.

Next, you must **rediscover your identity**. As I explained before, narcissistic abuse makes you feel lost and unsure of who you are. That's why you must find yourself again. Reconnect with the things you used to like – things that make you feel whole. Rediscover your values, interests, hobbies, skills, and activities you used to enjoy outside of a romantic relationship. Build a community of people who affirm your worth and cherish you. The moments you spend with them will be the building blocks of your new reality, one rooted in authenticity and self-worth.

Once again, you'll need boundaries to heal from the effects of gaslighting. The narcissist thrived on blurring lines and twisting your emotions. Once the relationship ends, learn to say no. Detach from conversations that feel toxic. Stay away from anyone who tries to pull you back into the fog. By this, I don't mean you should become cold or shut yourself off. Instead, recognize people who drain your energy or make you doubt yourself.

Rebuilding trust in yourself and others is a crucial part of healing from gaslighting. Here's how to do that:

- **Fact-check your thoughts**: When doubt creeps into your mind, write down the situation and accompanying negative thoughts. Then, challenge this thought with facts or evidence. What happened when you were in similar situations in the past? Did you turn out OK? Make a note of

every time you trusted your gut, and it paid off. This reinforces your intuition.
- **Journaling prompts**: Use prompts like "How did I get through past difficulties?" or "What does trusting myself in this situation look like?" to identify your strengths and limitations in rebuilding trust.
- **The "pause" button**: Before confiding in someone new, consider whether you've seen them keep other people's confidence or act with integrity.
- **Begin with small disclosures**: Only share small, non-critical information in the early stage of a new relationship. See how the person responds and whether they use the information against you.
- **The "circle of trust" exercise**: Draw circles on a piece of paper. In the innermost circle, write down people you completely trust. Gradually move outwards, adding people you trust with increasing levels of information.

Bonus: Therapy can be a powerful tool. A good therapist can help you identify lingering effects of gaslighting and develop healthy coping mechanisms. They can also provide a safe space to practice trusting another person.

Healing isn't linear. Some days will be full of clarity and moments of doubt that threaten to hurl you back into the fog. But each step you take will help you see the world more clearly. Eventually, you will reclaim your story, the narrative your abuser tried to rewrite. The fog will clear completely, revealing your strength and resilience.

Remember that narcissistic abuse doesn't define you. You're a survivor, and in time, you will regain the joy and confidence your abuser stole from you.

As we get closer to the end of this book, we must extensively discuss self-care. You cannot overstate the impact of self-care in healing and recovering from narcissistic abuse, especially as an empath. Even if you haven't fallen prey to a pathological narcissist, you still need self-care to stay recharged.

The next chapter is a dive into the world of self-care for empaths, so enjoy!

CHAPTER EIGHT:
Self-Care: Nurturing Your Empathic Soul

Self-care is essential for all empaths, regardless of whether they are in narcissistic relationships. It involves tending to the physical, emotional, mental, and spiritual aspects of one's life to promote health and wellness. Although it's sometimes mistaken for selfish indulgence, prioritizing self-care is crucial for overall well-being.

I meet many people who do not understand self-care. That's why this chapter aims to teach you what self-care is, how to practice it, and why you need it for optimal health and well-being.

The World Health Organization (WHO) defines self-care as "the ability of individuals, families, and communities to promote health, prevent disease, maintain health, and cope with illness and disability with or without the support of a healthcare provider." The WHO further explains that self-care is broad and involves different aspects of life.

My preferred definition of self-care is "a multidimensional, multifaceted process of purposeful engagement in strategies that promote healthy functioning and enhance well-being." Put another way, self-care means caring for yourself in ways that meet your physical and emotional needs.

All the healing and recovery techniques in the world won't help if you don't take care of yourself. Self-care is essential to balancing empathy and self-protection and preventing burnout. It involves recalibrating and reconnecting with your ability to relax, have fun, and bond with others healthily.

Good self-care takes different forms. It could mean getting adequate sleep every night or walking outdoors for a few minutes to enjoy nature. It could also mean investing time in activities that fill you with joy.

As an empath, you need self-care in different areas to restore balance and avoid emotional overload. Finding a balance that lets you address each area of your life is necessary to maintain your health and well-being.

To practice true self-care, you must use self-reliance and personal responsibility in a way that positively impacts your well-being.

What People Think Self-Care Is	What Self-Care Is
• Overindulgent spending	• Putting one's physical and mental health first
• Partaking in activities with instant gratification	• Embracing a healthy lifestyle in the long term
• Binge-eating favorite junk foods	• Following a healthy diet
• Having expensive spa days	• Working out regularly
• Going on lavish vacations	• Getting the recommended hours of sleep nightly
• Binge-watching movies and TV shows	• Taking time to participate in healthy activities that bring one joy
• Perfecting one's looks by all necessary means	
• Numbing unpleasant feelings with alcohol or other substances	• Treating any existing condition accordingly

In the short term, regular self-care practice can reduce stress levels, increase self-worth and self-esteem, and give you a sense of belonging. This is great for recovery because it improves overall emotional and mental health.

While the short-term benefits are good, the long-term ones are even better. Practicing self-care daily can improve conditions like anxiety, depression, diabetes, and heart disease. Other benefits include:

- Healthier relationships
- Reduced susceptibility to emotional overload
- Decreased burnout
- Better quality of life

- Higher job satisfaction

The question is, how do you practice self-care?

Best Self-Care Practices for Well-Being

Different aspects of life require self-care, each involving various activities and actions. None is more important than the other. You need all types to promote optimal health and well-being in all facets of life.

Physical

This is the type of self-care we learn to prioritize early in life. Physical self-care is vital for a good quality of life. It also helps to manage or prevent chronic health conditions. Every individual will take a unique approach to taking care of their physical health, but general practices include:

- Getting an adequate amount of exercise regularly.
- Eating healthy and well-balanced meals and staying hydrated.
- Getting proper sleep.
- Going for regular medical and dental examinations.
- Engaging in relaxing activities to manage stress.

Mental

You need mental self-care to nurture a healthy mind. Additionally, it assists in managing stress and anxiety, increases energy levels, and diminishes the likelihood of mental illness. Mental self-care involves practicing activities that stimulate your brain and engaging in functional behaviors. No two people are the same, but these strategies will help anyone take care of their mind:

- Try meditation, muscle relaxation, yoga, or breathing exercises daily.
- Read books and solve puzzles.
- Practice gratitude each day.
- Work out daily.

Relationships

A healthy relationship is a social form of self-care. Different types of relationships, whether platonic, familial, or romantic, all benefit from self-care. On the flip side, dysfunctional relationships are detrimental to health and well-being. Ways to practice relationship self-care include:

- Regularly getting together with friends and family.
- Volunteering at a local charity.
- Connecting with interest-based groups and communities.
- Joining a faith-based group for empaths.

Spiritual

As an empath, you must nurture your spirit to connect on a deeper level with yourself and the world. Some spiritual self-care practices include:

- Meditating
- Mindfulness
- Listening to soothing music
- Attending virtual spiritual activities for empaths
- Spending time in nature
- Getting a spiritual advisor who's also an empath

Here's a sample daily self-care routine incorporating energy protection, mindfulness, and emotional well-being.

Sample Daily Self-Care Routine

Morning (5-10 minutes)

- **Grounding (5 minutes):** Set your alarm 5 minutes earlier and spend that time in bed focusing on your breath. Breathe deeply in through your nose for a count of 4, hold for a count of 7, and slowly exhale through your mouth for a count of 8. Repeat this for 5 minutes.
- **Set Intentions (3 minutes):** While still lying in bed, visualize yourself throughout the day feeling calm and collected. Imagine yourself handling situations with empathy but maintaining your emotional stability.

Midday (15-30 minutes)

- **Digital Detox (30 minutes):** Schedule a break in your calendar for 30 minutes around lunchtime. Set your phone to silent and disable notifications on your computer. Take a walk outside, grab a healthy lunch in a quiet area, or read a book that has nothing to do with work.
- **Energy Check-in (5 minutes):** During your break, find a quiet spot and close your eyes. Notice if your shoulders are tense, your jaw is clenched, or your chest feels heavy. If so, take a few deep breaths, focusing on releasing tension with each exhale.

Evening (30-45 minutes)

- **Boundaries Review (15 minutes):** Before dinner, take some time to journal. Reflect on your interactions throughout the day. Did a conversation leave you feeling drained? Jot down the situation and brainstorm ways to set boundaries in similar situations in the future.
- **Creative Release (30 minutes):** After dinner, dedicate 30 minutes to an activity that allows you to express yourself creatively. This could be anything you enjoy, like painting, playing music, writing in a journal, or taking a dance class.
- **Relaxation Techniques (15 minutes):** Dim the lights in your bedroom and put on some calming music. Enjoy a warm bath with Epsom salts, engage in gentle stretching, or try progressive muscle relaxation. Tense and then relax different muscle groups, beginning from your toes and progressing upward.

Bonus: Throughout the day, whenever you feel overwhelmed, take a quick "sensory break." Step outside for a few minutes, close your eyes and focus on the sounds of nature, or smell a calming essential oil like lavender or chamomile.

Incorporating these practices consistently into your daily routine will help you master self-care for your protection and well-being.

Managing Overwhelm to Prevent Empathy Burnout

Burnout is an emotional drain caused by over-extending yourself without taking a break to recharge and replenish. Empathy burnout typically occurs when you've expended too much energy interacting with others. It also affects you after being repeatedly exposed to energy vampires.

Empathy burnout develops due to ongoing stress caused by constantly acting as an emotional crutch for others. Symptoms often include overwhelm, compassion fatigue, mental exhaustion, and low energy levels.

Being an empath puts you at a high risk of burnout due to your nature and the emotional demands that come with it. Caring for others while no one supports you is bound to cause overwhelm and exhaustion.

When overwhelmed or burnt out, you may encounter physical, mental, and emotional symptoms that might leave you feeling trapped in a state of brain fog. Fortunately, there are different ways to manage being overwhelmed and preventing burnout. These strategies are great for reducing the feeling of being overwhelmed daily and during particularly stressful moments.

Here's what to do when you notice overwhelm creeping on you:

- **Address the "why."** Determining the root of how you feel is a crucial first step. When you feel overwhelmed, ask yourself: Why do I feel this way right now? Once you identify the source, you're closer to solving the problem and improving your feelings.
- **Accept how you feel.** Don't ignore or deny that you're overwhelmed—that won't help. Dismissing it only bubbles the feelings under the surface until they spin out of control. Instead, accept that you're experiencing emotional overwhelm and acknowledge all negative thoughts. Do not judge yourself for having these thoughts or feeling this way. A non-judgmental approach is necessary to combat co-occurring feelings of guilt and shame.

- **Practice mindfulness.** When so many things are vying for your attention, it can be hard to focus on the present moment. But that's all you truly have. You can tune in and stay grounded in the present moment using mindfulness exercises. This will also reduce regrets over the past or anxieties about the future. Practicing mindfulness includes meditating, mono-tasking, yoga, dancing, etc.
- **Try a breathing exercise.** Deep breathing has been demonstrated to lower stress levels and improve mood. It can provide physiological and psychological relief, which makes it great for managing to overwhelm. When you feel overwhelmed, pause and take a few deep breaths, concentrating on your inhalations and exhalations until you begin to feel calmer.
- **Focus on things within your control.** Constantly worrying about things out of your control will only increase anxiety. It's best to focus on what you do have control over. When you think about something you can't change, gently redirect your attention to the one in your hands. Learning to let go of the uncontrollable will improve your life.
- **Color away the feelings.** Sometimes, it's tough to describe how you feel. The brain feels foggy. Coloring is a great way to seek relief in a fun activity. Grab a blank paper and get different colors of crayons—the more colorful, the better. Tune into your body, then choose a color that best expresses your feelings. You don't have to take a picture. Do whatever comes to you.
- **Ground yourself with the 5-4-3-2-1 technique.** This mindfulness technique engages your five senses to help you stay attuned to the present moment. You can use it to spontaneously ground yourself. To do it, look for 5 things in your environment and name them. Then, listen and label 4 sounds you can hear. Next, find 3 things you can touch and feel the textures. Then, notice 3 distinct smells and breathe them in. Finally, label 1 thing you can taste, such as the taste of a meal you just had.

With these tips, you can manage overwhelm and prevent burnout effectively.

Healthy Coping Mechanisms

Healthy coping mechanisms are tools for managing stress and difficult emotions constructively. They allow you to maintain control of your feelings and avoid resorting to habits that will only worsen your situation. You need healthy coping mechanisms to manage the daily influx of emotions and prevent overwhelmed and empathy burnout. You also need them to avoid compassion fatigue.

There are two types of healthy coping mechanisms:

- **Problem-focused:** These focus on the root cause of stress. Examples include boundary-setting, problem-solving, or seeking help from a professional.
- **Emotion-focused**: These address the emotions triggered by stress or overwhelm. They include relaxation techniques such as deep breathing, mindfulness, and progressive muscle relaxation.

Throughout this book, we've explored various problem-focused coping techniques that you can integrate into your daily life. Now, let's focus on emotion-focused coping skills, particularly relaxation techniques.

Common relaxation techniques include:

- Deep breathing
- Mindfulness
- Body Scan

One by one, we'll examine how you can practice each coping mechanism.

Deep Breathing

Choose a quiet place where you won't be interrupted. You have the option to sit upright in a chair or lie down on a yoga mat or bed. If you're sitting, make sure your feet are flat on the floor. Keep your legs straight, or if lying down, you can bend your knees for comfort. Additionally, loosen any tight clothing that may hinder your breathing.

Now, follow these steps:

1. Focus on your breath. Close your eyes gently, or soften your gaze if keeping them closed feels uncomfortable. Take a few moments to become aware of your natural breathing pattern.

2. Inhale slowly and deeply through your nose. Imagine you're filling your belly with air, not your chest. Feel your abdomen expand as you inhale.

3. Silently count to four in your head as you inhale. Then, hold your breath for a second or two at the peak of your inhale.

4. Exhale slowly through your mouth. Purse your lips slightly if you find it helpful. Slowly release the air from your belly, counting to six or eight as you exhale. Imagine you're releasing tension and stress with each exhale.

5. Continue this cycle of inhaling for four counts, holding for a moment, and exhaling for six to eight counts. Aim for several minutes of deep breathing, gradually increasing the duration as you become comfortable.

6. Pay attention to your body's sensations as you breathe. Feel your belly rise and fall with every breath. Don't force your breaths; breathe at a comfortable, natural pace.

Deep breathing is most effective when practiced regularly. Aim for a few minutes each day, even just a few cycles.

Mindfulness

This simple mindfulness exercise uses your five senses to ground you in the present moment. It's a great way to start your day or take a quick break to refocus whenever you feel overwhelmed.

Once again, sit or stand quietly so you won't be interrupted for a few minutes. Close your eyes gently or soften your gaze if keeping them open feels more comfortable. Then, follow these steps:

- **Begin with your breath.**

Inhale slowly and deeply through your nose several times, feeling your belly rise and fall with each inhale and exhale. Observe the innate rhythm of your breath without trying to control it.

- **Engage your senses.**

One by one, focus on each of your five senses. Here's what to explore with each:

1. **Sight**: What do you see around you? Notice colors, shapes, and textures. Are there any objects that hold your attention?
2. **Touch**: What can you feel? Feel your body against your clothing, your feet on the floor, or a hand resting on your lap. Notice the temperature and texture of what you're touching.
3. **Hearing**: What sounds can you hear, near and far? Pay attention to big and small sounds, like traffic outside or your breath.
4. **Smell**: Are there any scents you can detect? It could be coffee brewing, fresh air, or a hint of lotion.
5. **Taste**: Is there a taste present in your mouth? If not, notice the feeling of your tongue against your teeth or the inside of your cheeks.
- **Bring your awareness back.**

After focusing on each sense, take a moment to bring your awareness back to your breath. Notice how you feel now compared to when you began the exercise. You can repeat this exercise for a few minutes, focusing on each sense.

You can practice this mindfulness technique in everyday activities, like walking or eating mindfully.

Body Scan

This guided exercise will take you through a body scan, helping you relax and become more aware of your physical sensations. You can either sit or lie down, whichever feels most comfortable for you.

Step 1: Begin with Breath (2 minutes)

- Close your eyes gently, or soften your gaze if you prefer to keep them slightly open.
- Breathe in slowly and deeply through your nose and out through your mouth.
- Notice the rhythm of your breath. Don't try to force it; observe it.

Step 2: Scan Your Body (15-20 minutes)

- Now, direct your focus to the top of your head. Notice any sensations you feel there, like tightness, tingling, or warmth.
- Spend a few moments simply observing these sensations without judgment.
- Gently move your awareness down your face, neck, and shoulders. Notice any tension and allow it to soften with each breath.
- Continue scanning down your body, one section at a time. Pay attention to your arms, hands, chest, back, and abdomen. Notice any sensations of tightness, relaxation, or numbness.
- When you reach your legs, scan down to your feet, noticing any sensations in your toes and soles.

Step 3: Bring Awareness Back (2 minutes)

- Once you've scanned your entire body, take a few moments to become aware of yourself from head to toe.
- Notice how your body feels as a whole. Is it relaxed? Tense? A combination of both?
- Continue breathing deeply and slowly.

Wiggle your fingers and toes when you're ready, gently bringing your awareness back to the room. Practice this body scan regularly for the best results.

CHAPTER NINE:
Developing Resilience Against Setbacks And Failures

Picture a bouncy ball. It could be the type you used to play with as a child. Remember what happened when you dropped it? It would hit the ground and then bounce right back up. Sure, each bounce may not go as high up as the last, but it keeps bouncing.

Resilience works the same way. We all experience challenges and setbacks in life, just like the ball hitting the ground. Falling in love and entering into a relationship with a narcissist is a great example of such setbacks. But resilient people know how to pick themselves up, learn from the unpleasant experience, and focus on moving forward. They might not reach the same height as before, but they certainly don't let themselves remain on the ground. Instead, they keep bouncing.

As an empath and a narcissistic abuse survivor, resilience helps you to rebuild your sense of self and believe in yourself again. Healing takes time and effort. You will have moments of doubt and setbacks. But if you develop resilience, you can persevere through the healing and recovery process like it's not a big deal. It helps to trust your judgment and remain grounded while working through the aftermath of an abusive relationship.

Moving forward also means setting boundaries and possibly facing conflict. You need resilience to face these situations assertively and powerfully.

We all need resilience because life inevitably throws curveballs at us. As such, we need flexibility and strength to overcome the hurdles to success.

Here's why resilience is such a valuable asset:

- **Overcoming setbacks**: Everyone faces challenges, setbacks, and failures. Resilience helps us bounce back from these experiences, learn from them, and keep moving forward with a positive outlook.
- **Mental and emotional well-being**: Resilience is key to cognitive and emotional health. It aids in managing stress, anxiety, and depression, and fosters a sense of well-being even during challenging times.
- **Growth and development**: Challenges can be growth opportunities. When we face them head-on with resilience, we develop new skills, gain confidence, and become stronger individuals.
- **Healthy relationships**: Life throws challenges at our relationships, too. Resilience helps us weather storms in our personal and professional connections, fostering stronger bonds and better communication.
- **Adapting to change**: The world is constantly changing, and resilience allows us to adapt to these changes more easily. We can learn new things, adjust our plans, and embrace new opportunities.

In essence, resilience equips us to deal with whatever life throws our way. It allows us to survive and thrive in the face of adversity. You can see why it's a vital life skill.

Building resilience is a journey, but there are some great steps you can take to become more adaptable and bounce back from challenges.

Focus on self-care

This may seem redundant, but it's crucial. Prioritizing your physical and mental well-being helps you build a solid foundation for effectively managing stress. Make sure you prioritize adequate sleep, nourishing meals, and regular exercise. Remember to carve out time for activities you find enjoyable, whether it's reading, immersing yourself in nature, or spending time with loved ones.

Develop a positive outlook

Our thoughts significantly impact how we experience challenges. Try to cultivate a more optimistic mindset. Focus on the things you can control and reframe negative situations into opportunities for growth.

Build strong relationships

A supportive network of family and friends is a major buffer against stress. Surround yourself with positive people who believe in you and will pick you up when you're down.

Learn from setbacks

Don't see failures as the end of the road. Instead, view them as learning experiences. Analyze what went wrong and what you could have done differently, and use that knowledge to move forward with more confidence.

Practice healthy coping mechanisms

When you feel overwhelmed, it's important to have healthy ways to manage your stress. Activities like mindfulness, deep breathing exercises, body scans, or time in nature can all be helpful.

Develop problem-solving skills

Building your problem-solving skills allows you to approach challenges with a sense of control. Break down large problems into smaller, more manageable steps. Research solutions, brainstorm ideas, and don't hesitate to ask for help when needed.

Resilience is like a muscle that strengthens with exercise. Therefore, consistency is key to developing the strength and flexibility to bounce back from anything life throws your way.

Resilience Worksheet

Instructions: This worksheet will help you develop a more positive mindset and resilience when facing challenges. Take some time for yourself to complete each section thoughtfully.

List 3 things you are good at:

1. _____

2. _____

3. _____

Recall a time when you used these strengths to overcome a challenge. Briefly describe the situation and how your strengths helped you navigate it:

[   ]

- Reframe challenges:
1. Think of a current challenge you are facing. Briefly describe it here:

[   ]

Now, reframe this challenge as an opportunity for growth. How can you learn from or use this situation to develop new skills?

[   ]

- List 3 things you are grateful for today, big or small:

1. _____

2. _____

3. _____

Reflect on how gratitude can help you maintain a positive outlook even during difficult times.

[   ]

- Write down 3 positive affirmations for yourself. These affirmations should be phrased in the present tense and focus on your strengths and capabilities.

1. _____
2. _____
3. _____

- Here are some examples to get you started:
    - "I am capable of handling difficult situations."
    - "I am resilient and bounce back from setbacks."
    - "I learn and grow from my challenges."

Remind yourself of these affirmations daily, especially when you encounter challenges.

- Identify a role model who inspires you with their resilience. Briefly write about what you admire about them:

Developing resilience takes time and practice. With this worksheet, you can develop a more optimistic outlook and the strength to bounce back from any challenge life throws your way.

CONCLUSION

Being an empath isn't always easy. It means experiencing a world that can feel tough and unfriendly at times. But there's something special inside you – a powerful ability to deeply understand and connect with others.

This journey through "The Only Empath and Narcissist Bible" has given you the tools and knowledge to turn your vulnerabilities into strengths. You've learned how to set limits, protect your energy, and be kinder to yourself. Now, you can handle the ups and downs of relationships, knowing who truly cares about you and who might take advantage of your kindness.

Remember, empathy isn't a weakness; it makes you who you are. It lets you spread kindness and empathy wherever you go. By taking care of yourself, you attract good people who support you.

Balancing empathy and self-protection is something you'll keep learning. But with every step, you grow stronger and more confident. Embrace your special qualities, and remember, the world needs your empathy, but it's important to take care of yourself too. Keep moving forward, creating a beautiful balance where empathy and self-care work together perfectly.

Printed in Great Britain
by Amazon